T0352610

SPIRITUALITY FOR THE INDEPENDENT THINKER

Spirituality
FOR THE
INDEPENDENT
THINKER

THEMES OF RELIGIOUS
EXPLORATION

RICHARD STRINER

FIRST HILL BOOKS
An imprint of Wimbledon Publishing Company Limited (WPC)

This edition first published in UK and USA 2021
by FIRST HILL BOOKS
75–76 Blackfriars Road, London SE1 8HA, UK
or PO Box 9779, London SW19 7ZG, UK
and
244 Madison Ave #116, New York, NY 10016, USA

British Library Cataloguing-in-Publication Data
A catalogue record for this book is available from the British Library.

Library of Congress Control Number: 2021946519

ISBN-13: 978-1-83998-125-8 (Hbk)
ISBN-10: 1-83998-125-3 (Hbk)

This title is also available as an e-book.

CONTENTS

PREFACE

This book is not for everyone.

But it might appeal to people who refuse to be told what to think about religion. Those who rebel against the faith in which they were raised will tend to look for new alternatives—new ways of thinking and perceiving.

This book is for people like them.

They will experiment. They will sample the doctrines of other religions, and perhaps they will find themselves "converted"—especially if they happen to go through a mystical experience. Others will go on trying and discarding one religion after another until they reach the point where they find themselves content to formulate *their own* unique brand of religion—or irreligion.

In fact, when they reach this point, they may find that they are *more* than just "content" to think for themselves. They may find that they will *only* accept an approach to religion that is *their own.*

Entirely their own and not in any way inherited or "given."

Others will find that the comfort provided by their long-accustomed routine is too precious to renounce. So they will compromise—they will take their religion with a grain of salt, but they will cling to their old and inherited tradition as a way of life they need to retain. They will not break away from it completely.

A hilarious comedy routine about religion called "Letting Go of God" was produced in the 1990s by a star of the hit show *Saturday Night Live*, Julia Sweeney, who approached her subject with irreverence mixed with reminiscence. She recounted the process that led her to *question* the religious doctrines that others put forth with such confidence. And she found every one of them absurd.

She felt guilty and bad for a while, but then she came to the conclusion that *if* a god exists, that deity would probably *want* her to use all the brains and the intellectual initiative that she has been ... "given." And that permitted her to ... "let go." She flirted with atheism at first, but in time she declared herself to be a "naturalist" who looks to the honesty and candor of science as the surest guides to spirituality.[1]

For she remained spiritual. She was imbued with the feeling that the *mystery* of existence is inspiring enough to serve us as a source of profound spirituality for those who can appreciate it.

Spirituality derives from a combination of thinking and feeling—which is always the case when it comes to the mind's operations. This book rests upon the conviction that religious feelings should be *tested*—tested through critical analysis.

So I will take the reader into some issues of philosophy that may be unfamiliar at first. And these sections of the book require patience.

Religious propositions must be thought through carefully and well. But this should never be tedious. The issues themselves are so compelling that their exploration can be dazzling. Before very long, the exploration may assume the dimensions of a spell-binding *quest*—and I will seek to make the themes that are explored in this book as vivid as possible.

Abraham Lincoln reminisced in the very last months of his life about the penchant for analysis that he developed at a very early age:

> I remember how, when a mere child, I used to get irritated when anybody talked to me in a way I could not understand [...] I can remember going to my little bedroom, after hearing the neighbors talk of an evening with my father, and spending no small part of the night walking up and down, and trying to make out what was the exact meaning of some of their, to me, dark sayings. I could not sleep, though I often tried to, when I got on such a hunt after an idea, until I had caught it.[2]

Even abstruse points of theology can be rendered intelligible—if we *care*.

And religious issues are very much worth taking on—for ourselves and for others. So before proceeding further, I must share a few reflections on an ethical issue that takes the form of a dilemma.

We seek all we can to live up to our own best principles and practice what we preach. So if we choose a life of freedom when it comes to "matters of the spirit," we must extend to others the respect we will demand for ourselves. Toleration requires us to live and let live in matters of religion. But what if the religious doctrines of others make them persecute people like us?

What then? Should we ... "tolerate" them?

Naturally we have to resist them. But is it right to go further and point out to them that the doctrines that lead them to persecute others are grounded in notions that appear to be ... absurd? Are we respecting the freedom of others if we urge them to *free themselves* from the dogmas that we think are enslaving them? Are we succumbing to the ways of persecution ourselves when we engage in such behavior?

There may be no way around this dilemma in extreme situations, so we might as well admit it. The defense of the principle of freedom is sometimes a delicate challenge—a balancing act that requires us to summon all the conscience we have if we believe in the things that we espouse.

I am quite judgmental when it comes to basic human rights. I am tolerant *up to a point* when it comes to religious views of others, but my toleration lapses when the views and behavior of others lead to tyranny.

I am referring not only to tyranny in regard to the needs of other people but also (at times more insidious) to the mental tyranny that can stifle one's own legitimate needs.

Yes, there is surely a *presumption* here that I hope is not unduly *presumptuous*. I look upon freedom as *good*, and I *do* recommend it to others. For those whose emotional needs have been prompting them to cling to inherited ways, I seek to be respectful—*up to a point*. But I admit that I am prompted to challenge such people to empower and liberate themselves by giving their doctrines a good hard look by the standards of the "God-given" power that their own minds possess.

My mission is similar to that of Julia Sweeney, but I seek to go further. I seek to apply the methods of science and philosophy to issues of religion and spirituality that lead us to mystery—and then derive from it feelings that are useful to a life of spiritual awareness and spiritual freedom.

I advocate a certain procedure that is (or seems to be) necessary for such freedom. That method, as previously stated, is to take religious feelings and test them according to our higher powers of analysis.

Religious feelings will lead us by necessity to theories that need to be examined—thought through. Only after we examine our theories—and the feelings that prompt them—can we channel our instincts into ways of living that we trust.

Around the same time that Julia Sweeney was becoming influential, the vastly influential writer Karen Armstrong (of whom more will be said in due course) was advocating a different form of liberation. In her view, religion goes wrong when it takes any thoughts or doctrines pertaining to God in dogmatic terms—and especially in *literal* terms—instead of concluding that the only sane approach to spirituality is through imaginative experiences that may very well generate myths, which are all well and good provided that the myths are acknowledged to be *myths*, since the truth is unattainable.

I must confess to mixed feelings in regard to the prescription of Armstrong, since myths are quite admissible in literature and in art, if we use them as a source of entertainment or vicarious pleasure. Like millions, I enjoy the new myths that were created by J. R. R. Tolkien, especially for their extremely entertaining (and extremely unconvincing) religious content. I enjoy reading Homer and Virgil for similar reasons, and I sometimes enjoy the contemplation of works that are totally alien to any way of life that I would choose for myself. Even if I find their contents repugnant, my mental life has been strengthened by the fact that I encountered them. This is strictly a matter of *art* and the history of *art*.

But when myths are directly applied to a spirituality that is meant to be taken seriously, it is hard to avoid slipping into the literalism that Armstrong distrusts.

Distinguished theologians, philosophers, and religious commentators share Armstrong's view. They argue that myths can be used to express some important and compelling themes, and if used that way, they are good for the practice of religion. I understand this view, but it fails to mitigate the danger of mythological thinking.

A hair's breadth of difference stands between myth as a literary form—in other words, myth as an expression of *fiction*—and myth as the basis for theological *doctrine*, which can lead the susceptible to look upon fables as equivalent to *facts*. This happens all the time in fundamentalism. We see it in the words and the actions of all the enforcers of religious orthodoxy.

Consequently, I regard the application of myth to religious practice as extremely dangerous. I think that people are far better off if they can free their minds from the power of myth when there are serious issues at stake.

The problem becomes more complex if one moves beyond the three monotheistic religions that preoccupied Armstrong—Judaism, Christianity, and Islam—and considers the mythology of Eastern religions like Hinduism. In his book *The Tao of Physics*, Fritjof Capra observed that myths in the Hindu tradition are used metaphorically—they represent issues that are hard to articulate—and that myths of this type can be useful. He suggested that the dance of the Hindu god Shiva relates to the "cosmic dance" that physicists study in the field of quantum mechanics.[3]

And what can one reply to such comparisons?

Just this: I reiterate my point that the power of myth may be—I do not say "must" be—abused. Perhaps my view could be dismissed as the product of "Western rationalism," but one of the excellent points that Capra made in his book is that the celebrated "wisdom of the East" makes abundant provision for rationality: hence the famous dualism in China between Confucianism, which deals with problems that are readily intelligible, and Taoism, which deals with the ineffable.[4] I will have much more to say in due course about mysticism and the ineffable.

Indeed, I will explore the kinds of religious problems that can leave the power of "rationalism" speechless in the face of pure *wonder*. Just the same, the protocols of rationality are important. Mysteries of "the spirit" are just as real when encountered through critical analysis as they are when confronted via meditation.

And my suspicion of "myth" must remain.

Here again, I tread a very fine line when it comes to the fundamental issue of toleration. But I am free (in America, at least) to say exactly what I wish, and if my views about the role of myth in religion prove offensive to others, they should certainly make use of their God-given freedom to tell me so (respectfully, if possible).

Yet another form of religious liberation has been offered by spiritual teachers such as Eckhart Tolle and John C. Bader, who urge those in search of independence to "deconstruct" traditional religions with their bossy rules and their unconvincing dogmas and find their own spirituality in the "present moment." Tolle's book *The Power of Now* won a mass readership with this message. I have reached my own conclusion regarding "the power of now" that I will explain—sequentially—in this book. In a crucial respect I differ with Tolle and the others because—and this is a perennial problem in intellectual life—I believe that they have taken their doctrine too far.

I agree that the experience of "now" can be a powerful source of spirituality. I regard it as *the most inherently trustworthy* path to sane spirituality that we can explore. But Tolle and his colleagues often say that we should *turn away* from contemplations of the past and the future—contemplations that are often fraught with guilt, remorse, anxiety, or fear. And that, in my opinion, makes the path to independent spirituality much too simple. Why? Because it throws away chances to enrich our own lives and those of others by *shaping* the future in a way that will make the world better.

My work in Lincoln scholarship is grounded in my own firm belief—a belief that my experience confirms every day—that *strategic thinking* can change the world through the fine art of power orchestration. Strategic thinking can be used to create new ways for the future to unfold. And even though destructive people use the very same art to make things worse for everyone, that is all the more reason for people like ourselves to be masters of the art to defend the things we hold dear.

Only a deft understanding of the present moment as it verges strategically into ever-newer things can become the basis for strategic thinking—the basis for conceptualizing *over the horizon* to deliver the outcomes we want.

This book is an invitation to probe some emotional as well as intellectual dimensions of religion. The chapters take you down paths I have taken myself while acknowledging other possibilities. There is an argument that pervades this book, a point of view that emerges sequentially. Some of its themes will be clear at the outset, while others will emerge in due time. Too hasty a disclosure would rob this book of something vital: its power to surprise.

So be patient.

If the conclusions that I reach are of use to other people, so be it. But my conclusions are nothing more than thoughts that will have to be adapted—or questioned or modified—by everyone who chooses to consider them.

CHAPTER 1

TOWARD A SPIRITUALITY OF INDEPENDENT THINKING

Organized religion at its best can be the source of good things. When it leads to altruism—to charity and mercy—it can be a civilizing force. At its best, it provides a kind of comfort and consolation to the stricken. The beauty and the pageantry that accompany some of its rituals—especially its music, its architecture, and its other stimulations of the senses—can provide believers with a rich emotional and artistic source of sustenance.

But any or all of these benefits can be brought about in other ways. And the price to be paid for the occasional benefits of organized religion must be duly considered if we wish to lead lives of intellectual and emotional freedom.

For believers in organized religion are not fully free, they have stunted their powers of critical analysis through loyalty to a set of beliefs that were foisted upon them by others. To some extent they have given up the power to think for themselves.

There is no way around this uncomfortable and unhappy truth: members of organized religions are essentially allowing other people to tell them what to think. With the partial exception of modern creeds like Unitarian Universalism, which encourage people to think for themselves—and the exception here is partial because Unitarian culture often carries with it certain secular and political preferences that may tend to stifle maverick thinking—organized religion is a kind of mental tyranny.

Such tyranny becomes overt, extreme, and particularly hideous in cases where orthodox creeds are enforced by the state using threats of torture and death. Even at this late date in world history, this shameful spectacle is there for all the world to see and especially so within the Middle East. Such has been the way of religion at its worst throughout recorded history: whippings, mutilations, and burnings at the stake have been the fate of the courageous souls who dared to question or rebel. And the terroristic enforcement of religion is deepened by threats of eternal torment in the hereafter.

Persecutions, enforced conversions, and the brutal destruction of cultural monuments present a sorry spectacle that has spread itself over millennia. The cruelties inflicted on blameless individuals were terrible enough, but the destruction of art and culture must not be overlooked in an assessment of organized religion at its worst.

Early Christians destroyed all the literary evidence of early Norse religious culture except some fragmentary works that survived: Beowulf and the Icelandic Eddas. Spanish Catholics destroyed the works of Mayan religion except for some fragmentary writings. The Islamic Taliban recently destroyed ancient Buddhist statues in Afghanistan.

It is entirely possible that early Christians were the ones who destroyed the magnificent statue of Athena that Phidias sculpted for the Parthenon. No one knows for sure, but it would have made sense: she would have represented a "demon."

Many—perhaps most—members of organized religions were indoctrinated into their faiths as children. After being raised in accordance with the tenets of inherited orthodoxy, it is difficult for many to establish any mental autonomy in adulthood, except for occasional, private, and heterodox musings that are often accompanied by guilt. The quiet little tragedies of lives that are stunted by the petty strictures of dogma unfold every day. For those who never question and never feel prompted to question, religion is nothing better than a habit, a reflex, a ritualistic obedience to the ways of ancestors.[1]

The great American nineteenth-century-agnostic Robert Ingersoll wrote some grimly amusing reflections on the lives of such people. "Heredity," he wrote, "is on the side of superstition. [...] If we are to follow the religion of our fathers and mothers, our fathers and mothers should have followed the religion of theirs," and "had this been done, there could have been no improvement in the world of thought. The first religion would have been the last."

Obedience to the ways of ancestors is augmented by obedience to the ways of the culture or tribe. "The average man," wrote Ingersoll, "adopts the religion of his country, or, rather, the religion of his country adopts him. [...] It fits him because he has been deformed to fit it. [...] To him the religions of other nations are absurd and infamous, and their gods monsters of ignorance and cruelty." Never does it seem to occur to such believers that their own religion is viewed in the very same way by the followers of most other creeds.

Indeed, a sense of irony and hypocrisy seems to be temperamentally absent from the sensibilities of such people: "Thousands of missionaries," Ingersoll observed, "are sent to heathen countries to persuade the believers in other religions not only to examine their own superstitions, but to renounce them, and to adopt those of the missionaries."[2]

It is impossible for missionaries to regard their own creeds as superstitions, since they have long since lapsed into what Eric Hoffer once called "True Believers," the sorts of people who try to let orthodoxies do their thinking for them, people who invest their whole sense of selfhood in a belief system to which they surrender themselves with euphoria.

Superstitions and myths are the foundations upon which most organized religions have been built. The proverbial leap of faith is more often than not a leap downward, a leap into bondage, a leap into a pit of accumulated "old wives' tales" that dominate the mind and warp the process of thought.

Of course there is all the difference in the world between the sensibilities of fundamentalism—primitive, simplistic, and dictatorial—and the reflective ways of the multitudes of people who choose, for sentimental reasons, to maintain an allegiance to their ancestral creed while at one and the same time regarding its purported "revelations" as themes to be taken with a grain of salt, to be regarded as metaphorical or symbolic or poetic—themes, in short, that should not be taken literally.

Such is the case with the many variations of what some have called "liberal" Christianity.

There is nothing particularly new about this seemingly "modern" approach to spirituality, for in the Middle Ages the Falsafah movement in Islam preached a flexibility consistent with philosophy and science. The same could be said to some extent about the Scholastic movement in Western Christianity and the Rabbinic teachings of Talmudic commentary in Judaism. By the high Middle Ages, the Islamic preacher Abu Ali ibn Sina (known in the West as "Avicenna") became renowned for this outlook, and the Celtic theologian Duns Scotus Erigena regarded biblical texts as akin to symbolic poetry. In Hinduism, a very old tradition views ancient myths as nothing more than pathways for seekers to use as they seek the way to "Brahman," the ultimate spiritual reality.

Nonetheless, in all faith traditions is a core of inherited ways that cannot and must not be renounced if believers wish to retain their identity as *participants* in the movement. There is a definite *limit* to the individuality of anyone who chooses to participate in inherited "faith traditions."

For many who regard themselves as "liberal" Christians, the more delicate teachings of Jesus—the ones that are embodied in the Sermon on the Mount—are what really matter and, if taken to heart, such teachings permit one to enjoy all the beauties of Christmastime, the tuneful carols, the family togetherness, the festive decorations, without getting too caught up in the theological principles that lie at the very heart of Christian orthodoxy.

But those principles—the "incarnation," the immaculate conception, the virgin birth—remain in place, and it is only an exercise of mental evasion that permits reflective people to avoid engaging with them in a serious and conscientious way. But engage with them we must if we wish to avoid a deep feeling of hypocrisy as we chant out the lyrics of the carols that perforce accompany the melodies we love so well.

So—we must confront the dogmatic and orthodox proposition that Jesus was both human and divine. He was supposedly the "son of God." Whence came this proposition? From the Gospels, say many believers, but we have no idea of who really wrote those accounts. "Tradition," and tradition alone, is invoked with regard to the authorship of "Matthew," "Mark," "Luke," and "John," just as Jewish tradition ascribes all five books of the Pentateuch to the authorship of Moses.

These are legends without a shred of proof.

We will never know who really wrote these ancient texts—or who might have revised them. Some scholars believe that the names of the putative Gospel-writers were only attached to these texts in the second century AD, long after the supposed authors were dead and gone. There is much that we know as a matter of historical fact in regard to the creation of early Christianity—especially the crucial role of St. Paul—but there is much that will never be known. What Jesus said and what he really claimed to be are in the final analysis anybody's guess, so it is useless to presume much of anything in these matters.

The bible on the whole is a hodgepodge of passages written by people who never identified themselves and who seemed in some cases—especially in the case of the Ezekiel sections and the book of Revelation—to have been suffering from hallucinations. Large portions of the Bible appear to be the work of busy zealots who inserted new doctrines into earlier passages in order to create a foundation—a spliced-together foundation—for their own ever-changing theology.

The most cursory study of ancient culture suggests that a process of "syncretism" was involved in the development of early Christianity, a blending of themes that converged in Judea from elsewhere. The culture of Greece was infused to some extent into ancient Judea in the "Hellenistic" period that followed the conquests of Alexander the Great. And Greek mythology was rife with stories of divinities fathering children with mortals: Heracles, for instance, the semi-divine son of Zeus, the son of a deity and the mortal woman Alcmene who was gifted with extraordinary powers and who was martyred and then resurrected—lifted to apotheosis, to live forever on Olympus with his father.

Consider too the cult of Dionysos, the god who dies and is resurrected in the springtime. In most versions of the myth, Dionysos was the son of Zeus and the mortal woman Semele—or Thyone in alternate versions. He dies and is gloriously reborn every year; he is the god of the vine whose resurrection is accordingly celebrated in the spring. From the myths of Dionysos came the ancient Greek cult of "Orphism," a belief system wherein Dionysos worship wafts the soul of the believer into life eternal.

A comparable cult of resurrection and life eternal was embodied in the Greek "Eleusinian Mysteries," based upon the tales of Demeter and Persephone, who is taken by the lord of death to the underworld (to be his bride) but is then resurrected every year. Participants in the Eleusinian Mysteries were assured that they, too, through participation in the cult, might gain life everlasting.

The theme of a resurrected god who holds the key to life eternal was perhaps imbibed by the Greeks from the Egyptian myth of Isis and Osiris, the latter a god who was slain and resurrected and whose worship is a rite of passage to the afterlife.

These comparisons are merely suggestive, but they hint at a definitively pagan dimension of early Christianity that modern believers should consider if they wish to lead lives of intellectual candor—and liberation.

And what has been said here about Christianity could be said with equal force in regard to the origins of other religions. Buddhism, for instance—perceived very often by seekers in the West as an alternative to the worst side of monotheistic religion—has its own mythological features, some of them sadistic, that have shaped its teaching to this day.

Many variations of Buddhism teach that the souls with bad karma will be taken to "narakas," or hells, and then stay there for millions of years before their next incarnations. Gods like "Yama" or "Enma" will torture these wretched souls for eons.

Naïve Westerners who idealize "Buddhism" are usually shocked when they learn of this doctrine.

The question has to be asked: Is it possible for people in the modern world to participate in festivals like Christmas—or to practice Eastern-style meditation—without allegiance to myth-based theology? Is it possible to consider the issues of spirituality in a manner that—in emotional as well as intellectual terms—is fully independent? Do we not deserve the *freedom* to do so if that is what we wish?

If so, what basis can we find for a spirituality of our own that is free from any shaping influence by organized religion?

By thinking independently—by allowing our power of *wonder* to flow where it will—by asking good questions, by following up with critical analysis, by learning from the best and most open-minded speculations of philosophers and scientists, we may begin to discover the basis for a new inner world.

The case can be made that by pondering the spirituality that is latent in some *facts about our everyday lives*—facts about our daily existence that we take completely for granted—and by exploring these themes in a way that is guided by the best speculations in philosophy augmented by the findings of up-to-date science, especially physics, we gain an outlook richer by far than any gratification to be found in most of the brittle, outmoded, and antiquated structures of myth-based conventional religion.

This outlook can only be derived from an exploration of spiritual values that embodies itself as a *quest*.

"BEING"

Our ability to explore religious issues on a rational and intellectual basis—instead of through dogma or even through mysticism—is governed by the mental process that we happen to possess and by the senses with which we are endowed. Any attempt to conceptualize what we might call "ultimate realities" depends upon the structures created by our minds. There is no way to sidestep this problem, which is simply a matter of biology. With the mental equipment that we have, there are severe limitations in regard to what our minds can do and know. We may in fact be no more capable of fathoming "ultimate realities" than a cold virus is capable of understanding this sentence.

Be that as it may, our minds will nonetheless create certain kinds of ideas in regard to what philosophers have called "metaphysics"—which might be defined as the speculative contemplation of the force (or forces) that underlie and constitute reality as we experience it. Nothing can be proven in regard to such matters, but, the human mind being what it is, our ruminations lead us to theories. When applied to religion, these theories are centered on the grounding of the universe.

For example, religious speculation has generated the following distinct kinds of theories: (1) "theism," the theory that a creative being exists who is distinct from the cosmos that he/she/it created; (2) "atheism," the theory that the cosmos itself is the only reality and that "supernatural" or "divine" force does not exist; (3) "pantheism," the theory that the cosmos itself is in some sense "divine;" and (4) "polytheism," the theory that multiple deities exist—or *could* exist.

None of these theories can be proven or disproven. In the eighteenth century, the Scottish philosopher David Hume had a great deal of fun in an essay entitled "Dialogues Concerning Natural Religion," setting forth the almost endless possibilities that religious speculation can lead to. The fictitious characters in Hume's "Dialogues" share all sorts of ideas: the idea that the universe was built by a bungling workman, that the universe is something of an unsuccessful experiment (the latest in a series), that the universe results from the inconsistent labors of several deities, that the universe is something like an animal (or a plant), that the creator of the universe got bored and walked away, leaving us to wonder what happened.[3]

Hume's essay is highly entertaining—so much so, in fact, that it can prompt us to shrug away such questions and dismiss religious issues from our minds. But another philosopher, William James, once observed that whenever he was tempted to imagine "that the world of sensations and of scientific laws and objects may be all," he heard "an inward monitor [...] whispering the word 'bosh.'"[4] Our instincts lead us to *believe* that metaphysical subjects deserve exploration since they bear upon the meaning of our lives. Perhaps we all have asked the following question:

Why does anything exist instead of nothing?

That was the question that philosopher Martin Heidegger used as the opening sentence of a book entitled *An Introduction to Metaphysics.*[5] And he was not the first philosopher to pose this question. Wilhelm Gottfried von Leibniz asked the question centuries earlier. And it was the centerpiece of disputation among the very earliest known philosophers, the pre-Socratics, though they generally did not pose the issue as a question.

The issue was "being"—the fundamental matter of what it means to "be" and the mystery of *how* things can "be."

That is not the sort of subject that most people think about routinely. We take it for granted that we and the things that surround us *exist* because we feel no reason in our day-to-day living to dwell upon the matter. But if we turn to religious reflections, the issue surges forward and we wonder "how the universe was created." This reveals a quirk in our mental process. When we think in grandiose terms about the fact that *the universe* exists, then the issue of being is fundamental. In our day-to-day reality, however, the issue is absent from our thoughts. Heidegger called this problem "forgetfulness of being."[6]

If we cease to be forgetful—if we take just a moment to dwell upon the nature of our everyday experience—another issue may confront us, the existence of *time.*

We know what we mean when we think about time itself: it is the process of flow in which experience unfolds in a sequence. We measure the passage of time and then we use it to regulate our lives. But if we ever take a moment to ask ourselves a very simple question, "What *is* it?" we reach an impasse.

Think for a moment about the fact that you are here, right now in this moment. This moment? And which moment precisely do you mean? As you think about the moment you are in, it goes away—it is lost in the past. Each moment (so-called) is melting backward in the on-flow of time. And what happened to the "you" that was thinking such thoughts? Where did it go? You are still the same "you," are you not? And yet you *aren't*, since the "you" that exists in this flickering "now" is not the "you" that existed just a moment before, in a reality that vanished into nothing.

Something ghostly—something uncanny—is unfolding all around us and within us, yet we seldom find it ghostly and uncanny. Until we take just a moment (or a series of moments) to *think*.

Think about the common science fiction fantasy of time travel, for example. It is based upon the presupposition that everything that ever happened to you or to anyone else is still "back there," intact, and that the things that all happened in the past are still in some sense (this point has to follow) *alive*. And yet how can that science fiction proposition be true? If the "you" that existed a moment ago is now *gone*, then the principle of time travel is absurd. But if that previous "you" is still "back there"—a very big "if"—how exactly does it go on "living?" Is everything that you ever did or thought being endlessly repeated by an infinite series of "selves?" And if so … "where" exactly is all of this happening? If the past still "exists," where exactly does it still possess "being?"

Saint Augustine in the course of his *Confessions* proclaimed that "if the past and the future do exist, I want to know where they are." Indeed, while we are measuring time, he observed, we ought to ask ourselves some mind-expanding questions like these: "Where is it coming from, what is it passing through, and where is it going?"[7]

The ancient Greek philosopher Parmenides came to the conclusion (so far as we can reconstruct his views from the fragments of his writings that survive) that the process of change and flux is an illusion. Heraclitus, however, reached the opposite conclusion and decided that *becoming*, not "being," was the essence of the cosmic process.

Plato was fundamentally troubled by the fact that the reality we know is so fleeting and insubstantial, every moment lapsing constantly into nonentity. At the very instant it unfolds in the flickering "now," that reality is *gone*. He decided that a higher and separate realm of "being" must exist—a realm of perfect, eternal, unchanging "Ideas" that form the models upon which our lower and fallen and flickering world must be based, however imperfectly.

Centuries before Plato, Heraclitus, or Parmenides, one of the authors of the Hindu Upanishads explored the unavoidable paradoxes of what philosophers call the subject of "ontology" (the study of the nature of being itself) in relation to the mysteries of cosmology and primal creation:

> Initially being alone existed.
> Being only and without a second.
> Some say that in the beginning, nonbeing alone existed.
> Non-being, only nonbeing, without a second.
> And from this nonbeing, being will proceed.
> But in truth where could it be so?
> How could being proceed from nonbeing?
> One must think that being alone exists, being only and without a second.[8]

In the twentieth century, philosophers, mystics, and scientists explored the many hidden dimensions of the problems of "being" and "becoming." A review of their theories sheds light upon a fact of our everyday world that those who seek a form of "natural religion" may regard as a clue: the existence of "now."

CHAPTER 2

METAPHYSICS, PHYSICS, AND THE SPIRITUALITY OF *NOW*

The mysteries of "being" and "becoming" are integral to science—especially to physics—but the findings of current-day physics make the mysteries in some respects deeper than ever as we seek to apply them to everyday experience.

So we might as well consider the issue of whether or not the most advanced findings (or theories) of science really *can* be relevant to everyday spirituality. The case can be made that the connection is important—even vital—and that the most paradoxical issues that are raised by science are no more challenging in their way than the comparable issues of abstract theology, for those who take the time to consider them.

Science and spirituality are governed by the same limitations: the limitations of the human mind and its power to conceptualize.

So the mysteries confronting the spiritual seeker are matched, in some cases, by mysteries of science, and such mysteries have tended to converge in the field of cosmology. It should not be surprising that theology and cutting-edge physics have arrived at some similar conundrums.

A long time ago, the universe that the atheists (or the "materialists") envisioned was a simple affair: it consisted of physical particles in empty space, and it was governed by the mathematical principles of Newton. But in the twentieth century, relativity theory and quantum mechanics forced scientists to confront a more paradoxical universe. Today, instead of thinking of a universe of particles that bounce around in empty space, we think of a "space-time fabric," and this fabric is a very strange thing—especially so if the findings of quantum mechanics are considered.

The field emerged in the early twentieth century when scientists discovered that light waves sometimes take on the qualities of packet-like "quanta" of energy, that is, "particles." They also discovered that particles can sometimes behave like waves, which means that a particle/wave duality exists. Gradually

11

the concept of "quantum field theory" developed, with quanta being understood as "excitations" of underlying "fields."

A whole new vocabulary developed, and its terms have continued to challenge the lay public. Even scientists will sometimes employ the old term "particle" as a shortcut, for simplicity's sake. What they are really talking about are pulses or *tendencies* or *actions* in the subatomic realm.

Werner Heisenberg discovered that the motions of quanta are highly irregular—to put it mildly. They move and behave in a manner impossible to measure with consistent precision and they seem to have a wildness and indeterminacy in their very nature.

Moreover, the act of observing them seemed, in a weird sort of way, to affect them. This astonishing fact was confirmed beyond doubt through experiments. The Danish physicist Niels Bohr joined Heisenberg and others in advancing these extraordinary findings. Together, they argued that an indeterminacy is built into the very fabric of nature. The phrase "quantum weirdness" began to make the rounds among the physicists.

Some took the mystery in stride for a very simple reason: the *usefulness* of quantum mechanics. For the field was generating mathematical tools that could predict some *large patterns*—in spite of the mystery.[1]

The extent to which quantum indeterminacy affects the large patterns of nature—especially in light of the majestic regularity and continuity that nature on the grand scale *appears* to possess—is a vexed question, since more and more physicists are certain that a "quantum cosmology" lurks in the seemingly dependable laws of the universe.

More on that later.

The most avant-garde principles of astrophysics and particle physics these days—principles embodied in what is currently called "string theory"—have led to even stranger suggestions. String theory holds that the constituent elements of the cosmos are one-dimensional objects—"string"—that may be coiled into loops or else extended in linear constructions. But there was more: the notion that reality encompasses far more dimensions than the three dimensions of space (and the one dimension of time) that we know.

Hidden dimensions.

One variation of the theory envisions the rotation of string-loops in *11-dimensional space*. This particular conception is microcosmic—it applies to the tiniest proportions. Other variations of the theory are macrocosmic: they envision much larger dimensions that *contain* the cosmos we inhabit. These macrocosmic dimensions were given the name of "branes" by the 1990s—with "brane" a derivative of "membrane." Different calculations have invested these objects with alternative dimensionalities.[2]

In addition to the concept of *spatial* dimensions that are hidden from us, there is also speculation about the existence of multidimensional time.

So our instinct to *picture* the cosmos as a place that exists within three-dimensional space must be discarded if the current theories are correct. Instead, we must contemplate the existence of a mysterious "fabric" that *generates* the qualities of space and time that we experience. But we must also remember that this fabric possesses spatial and temporal qualities that *we cannot experience.* We can never *experience* 11-dimensional space—or any other hidden aspect of space-time.

And "outside" of the cosmic space-time fabric there is ... what, precisely?

"Nothingness" is a quality that we can only postulate through inference— an abstraction. "Emptiness" refers to a quality of *space,* but no space can exist outside the fabric—or so it seems. So where does that leave us? At the edge of our conceptual powers. Even mathematics has its limits.

A similar problem of conceptualization arises when we contemplate the issue of how the cosmos "began." According to the "Big Bang Theory," the universe emerged in some cataclysmic fashion from a cosmic "singularity"— whatever that means. It appears there was no space or time before the "Bang." Our powers of abstraction are defeated if we try to understand the singularity.

It was a "thing" of some sort—that much is clear—and yet it lacked both extension and duration. So how did those particular qualities emerge from a thing that possessed neither one of them?

How did space and time emerge from such a state—a state that was spaceless and timeless? Even instantaneous events involve a *process* of sorts, do they not? If they didn't, they would not be *events.*

So how did the singularity explode into "Bang" without a sequence of before and after—time—in which the explosion could *be triggered,* in which it could "*happen*" and "come into being?" According to quantum theory, things like the singularity and the "Bang" simply ... *are,* and we will never know more.

Big Bang theorists argue that the singularity was a cosmic *compression* of infinite magnitude. To conceive of this, we must imagine the entire universe compressed to a point. Big Bang theorists believe that was just what it was. But if space and time did not exist in the point—it appears that they came "*later on*"— *how* did the explosion occur without at least the *potential* for time? How can we explain it?

We cannot.

The same conundrum confronts the theologians who argue that *God* caused the process of creation. A common point of doctrine in Christian theology is the proposition that God transcends the process of time: Saint Augustine wrote that he is "outside time in eternity."[3] Saint Thomas Aquinas wrote that God is immutable, eternal, and completely unaffected by time—he is "altogether unchanging."[4]

But how could God *do* anything if he is "outside" the sequence of time and "altogether unchanging?" How could he create the universe—indeed, how could he do anything at all? How can God *cause* things to happen without being somehow *within* a continuum that moves from "before" to "after?" Or else (alternatively) containing *within himself* a process of temporality, a possibility that seems to be moot if God is never subject to change.

There are other possibilities within the monotheistic tradition for conceptualizing God. A number of Christian theologians in the twentieth century acknowledged this. But the orthodox Christian version of theism—even with the escape clause of miraculous agency—leads straight to a conceptual dead-end.

The question of origins pushes the human mind to the limits of its power to conceptualize. We are left with the uncomfortable thought that our need to comprehend reality in terms of origins—and many people cannot let go of this impulse—is nothing but a biological quirk that renders us incapable of coming to grips with the possibility that "ultimate realities" transcend what we understand as "origins."

That is not a very new idea. Atheists for years have argued that the universe has "always existed" and a "Steady State" theory in physics—supplanted in the 1960s by the Big Bang theory—held much the same view. And even the Big Bang theory has some interesting loopholes that can lead us past the issue of origins.

Ever since the 1980s, when Stephen Hawking and James Hartle advanced a "No-Boundary" theory of the universe, physicists have struggled with the possibility that the universe had no origin *as such* but in some uncanny fashion "created itself"—or is "creating itself"—through some kind of quantum enigma.[5] And yet even that term—"creating itself"—may be a misnomer, since according to these particular theories, there is no necessity for any form of "creation."[6]

Perhaps the universe just "is." Perhaps it subsists in a manner that is *circular* or otherwise *continuous*. Or if the Big Bang occurred, it could be one in a series of Bangs (and rhythmic compressions that precede new explosions) that stretch backward in an infinite regress, backward into a mystery whose nature is far more profound than the mind can guess.

It could be part of a rhythm of expansion and contraction that never really... started, as we understand the term. It just "is." There is a strain of thought within the Buddhist tradition that supports this view. The cosmologists Paul Steinhardt and Neil Turok have embraced it in their book *Endless Universe*. If the vision is correct, then the laws of every universe derive at least in part from the previous one.

In the opinion of philosopher Thomas Torrance, "there is no intrinsic reason in the universe why it should exist at all, or why it should be what it actually is."[7] And yet our minds will always return to the nagging old question of "why."

If the "stuff" of the universe exists for some reason we can never comprehend, do the *laws* that govern its existence have a higher existence of their own? And if so, exactly *where* did the antecedent laws of physics "come from?" What is their ... *foundation*? Is there a reason behind the brute fact of existence, a reason from which the raw stuff of the cosmos may ... emanate?

This is the question that has tantalized the mathematical physicist Paul Davies for the past 30 years. He has sought to raise questions regarding the "agency" that is "somehow responsible for the laws of physics, which govern, among other things, how space-time evolves." What kind of a force, he inquires, can "breathe fire"—the phrase was coined by Stephen Hawking—"into the equations that encode the laws of physics?"[8]

We will revisit that very potent inquiry in subsequent chapters.

In the 1980s, another physicist, David Bohm, produced a theory that addresses these questions in an ontological manner. He suggested that a realm of "pre-space" contains the *possibility* for space and time: it is an "implicate order" where the embryonic forms of such things are "enfolded." The reality we know—the "explicate" order—is the place of "unfolding," and he argued that our cosmos is something like a holographic projection. Bohm, it bears noting, was deeply influenced by mysticism, and his theories took shape in conversations with the Dalai Lama.[9]

The link between the "new physics" and Eastern religions was established definitively in 1975 with the publication of *The Tao of Physics* by the physicist Fritjof Capra, and this link has been developed ever since.

So, can laymen extract any spiritual theme from cutting-edge physics—a theme with applications that apply in emotional and intellectual terms to the circumstances of our own lives?

Yes.

Every moment we experience life we see a truth that transcends every other. There is a power of *being* that is completely self-evident and nothing that we know can account for it. Settle if you wish for what the physicists call the singularity. In some way that our minds can never fathom, it generated *force* that we can feel every moment.

Let us call it the experience of *now*.

THE SPIRITUALITY OF *NOW*

The experience of *now* is a condition that people simply take in stride—for obvious reasons. And yet the simplest of things can be fraught with a numinous power—and interesting surprises.

So if we look at this condition that people take for granted and scrutinize it—*pay attention*—we may discover some things that are helpful to us in the quest for our own brand of spirituality.

Let us start with the matter of words—and definitions.

The concept of *now* is rather hard to explain in mere words if you consider all the issues. The words at our disposal have different connotations that demand to be probed and explored. What difference does it make if we decide to say "now" or "the present"— terms that we use every day? Their basic meaning might seem to be equivalent. But they are not in truth equivalent terms.

"The present" is a very bland term that does not really challenge our minds. It is descriptive. But *now* is a word that can be fraught with impressive forms of power. If we *shout* it—shout it at someone in the form of an imperative *command*—we are using it to bring about *change*. We are using a word that has a potent array of higher meanings, all of them *kinetic*—fraught with power.

The most potent of the meanings is the cosmic one, in which *now* becomes the most comprehensive: it means *everything there is* in this particular moment that will *never ever come again*. If you happen to be thinking of *now* in this way, there is a higher meaning in your thought—one that goes beyond what you typically mean if you are casually speaking of "the present."

And if you happen to be thinking of *yourself* in this connection, the stakes are raised even more. Close your eyes and recite the word *now*. A hush may fall over your mind as you contemplate *yourself* in relation to the vast and mysterious existence that *holds* you and *contains* you this instant—*this instant* that will never come again in all the rolling infinity of years.

That is *now* as an expression of a spiritual condition that we *feel*.

It is time for us to shift for a moment from these very strong emotions to a more analytical posture. For *now*, in the greater cosmic sense we have just been explaining, relates to *being* as a metaphysical problem and the intellectual dimensions of this problem should not be neglected.

Let us think for a while about *now* in the sense of a metaphysical "condition."

There are many different ways for us to think about the *now situation*—to probe it. We are *in* the situation we are trying to describe and, of course, this complicates the problem. We can take a few steps in the direction of a visualization that could help us to navigate the issues. Shall we draw a picture? It is helpful sometimes to be able to visualize things if we are just beginning to explain them.

The experience of *now* comes from *time*—or so it appears. The process of time has *contained* us somehow in a "moment" that can stretch into a *flow*. And that is *now* as a cosmic condition.

Just imagine the universal flow as a *wave* and you will easily visualize *now*. It is the *crest*. But this is merely a conceptual shortcut—a pretty picture. It is not, of course, a real explication.

We could visualize *now* as a presentational *field* that makes the whole world *immediate*. That's nice, and yet it doesn't really take us very far if we intend to move on to analysis. And so enough of pretty pictures for the moment: let us think about *now* more abstractly.

What *is* it—this *focus* of our world?

No one knows. Scientists have explored the situation sometimes in a tentative manner. Physicist Henry P. Stapp describes the structure of *now* as a "surface" that stands between—or mediates—the "space-time regions" corresponding to "the fixed and settled past" and "the potential future."[10]

For most of us, the existence of the *now* situation is simply a … "given." A mysterious condition that we have to accept, and yet it pushes our minds to reach out to their limits, for we urgently want to understand.

And that's *exactly* why this constitutes a spiritual challenge that rational people should pursue. If we take a good look at what's before our eyes this very moment—if we look at a condition that we always take for granted and *behold* it as we really ought to do—we could find a new mysticism we *trust*.

The existence of *now* is a mystery that physicists have sometimes tried to shrug away. Some of them call it an illusion that relates to the larger so-called illusion that time really "passes." Yes, you heard that correctly, for some people in the worlds of philosophy and physics have said it. More on that in the following chapter and later in the book. These are problems that physicists are ill-equipped to handle if they don't ask some ontological questions. And some don't.

But if we pay close attention to the theories of physicists who think *philosophically*, the mystery of *now* can be explored.

In light of the conceptual importance of this theme, it will be necessary in the pages that follow to discuss some very challenging issues. So consider this material with patience as you walk the new landscape.

As a figure of speech, we referred in the previous chapter to the "flickering 'now'"—flickering for us in the sense that its *content*s are always in motion. But there is a very different side to this question. The experience of *now* remains *steady* for us if we feel it as an ever-present *structure*, which, of course, we constantly do—a structure so basic that we probably (nay, certainly) take it for granted.

As Martin Heidegger put it, we experience *now* in the immediate and obvious sense of *"this* thing which changes," but we know it in a different sense as the thing that "simultaneously shows its own constant presence."[11] In this way, it exemplifies *both* of the two ontic states that philosophers consider: becoming and being.

In fact, it *synthesizes* them—a point of the utmost importance.

Relativity teaches us that "now" will be experienced differently in different parts of the cosmos. When speed is increased, a "dilation" or a "stretching out" of time results—time slows—and so the "now" of a person on a space ship will be different from the "now" of a person on Earth. But we have every reason to presume the pervasiveness as well as the factuality of *now*, do we not?

Perhaps not. Some physicists claim that our experience of *now* has been proven illusory by relativity. Because the curvature of space-time is warped— and this has been proven—there is no real "simultaneity." Moreover, the *feeling* that we have about time has not been proven by scientific methods. Listen to the physicist Paul Davies discuss these particular things:

> It is not merely the temporal flux that baffles us. The passage of time is often viewed as the progress of "the now" *through* time. We can envisage the "now"—being singled out as a little glowing point. As "time goes on," so the light moves steadily up the time line towards the future. Needless to say, physicists can find nothing of this in the objective world: no little light, no privileged present, no migration up the time line.[12]

The frustration is keen because the problem is very hard to study—for physicists or anyone. We cannot "step out" of the time-flow in order to *see* that little "light" and its "migration."

The problem is *ontology*—and not physics.

Toward the end of his life, Albert Einstein discounted the "illusion" of past, present, and future.[13] But his reflections on the subject were not at all consistent, if recorded evidence of private conversations may be trusted. He once supposedly mused that "there is something essential about the now"—something that lies "outside the realm of science."[14] Something that defies the human powers of conceptualization and makes our experience of *now* extremely cryptic.

Shall we explore it?

Stand back from the experience of *now* and then ask yourself what it means. It is a *fact* that never goes away. Should we see in it a signal that *existence* will never go away—a signal from afar? Should we view it as a kind of benediction—an affirmation that a world of some kind will always *be?*

Whatever it is, it is a fact with profound implications.

If *now* is pervasive, should we view it as the fundamental force that *allows* reality to be? Is reality from moment to moment *supported* by its ever-present power? Perhaps a phrase from *Deuteronomy* suggests the hidden meaning of *now* and the mystery behind it: "underneath are the everlasting arms."

It's like a *spell.*

The present slips away into the past, and we can *feel* the flow of time as it is moving. But we live in a dimension that can *penetrate* time and give the world its very essence and structure. We call it "now." The universe is fluid but the structure of *now* never varies—it stays the same.

So what is it?

Every instant that we live, we have a constant demonstration of the basis for natural religion.

CHAPTER 3

WHY IS THE WORLD THE WAY IT SEEMS?

If we open our minds to the spirituality of our existence—as exemplified by the mystery of *now*—we may see that this world of ours should not be taken for granted, even for an instant. When considered in its fullest dimensions it may suddenly appear to us a wondrous dispensation. The mathematician and philosopher Alfred North Whitehead stood back from the world and perceived it as something like a magic spell; "the concept of 'God,'" he once wrote, "is the way in which we understand this incredible fact—that what cannot be, yet is."[1]

The reality of being, as we ponder it more, should draw forth from us an almost boundless capacity for wonder.

And yet we come down to earth very quickly if we contemplate the darker side of things. Life can be cruel—unthinkably so—and the potentialities of nature, especially our own human nature, are rife with perverse possibilities. The carnivores are feeding on each other as we speak, and as we think of all the suffering and pain in the universe, we falter.

So we seek a sense of purpose in the universe to help us come to terms with all the pain. The search for *meaning* in the cosmos is called "teleology"—from the Greek word "telos," meaning goal—and sooner or later it is linked to the problem of evil.

Our wonder at the miracle of living—of existence—is tempered by our knowledge of the violence "mother nature" inflicts. *Why* does the miraculous cosmos contain so much savagery?

The polytheists have a very simple answer: multiple deities. These deities, they say, are at war with one another, and some of them are really quite nasty. "Dualists" make the matter even simpler: they envision an endless struggle between two opposite realms of metaphysical or supernatural force, good and evil, and the cosmos we are doomed to inhabit gets torn every day by their struggle.

Monotheistic religion makes things more complicated. The idea of one deity is simple enough, but the problem of accounting for the evil in his universe is not. Monotheists usually believe that their God is beneficent. So why does He allow so much evil to exist—especially if his power is said to be "omnipotent?" Attempts among theologians to solve this problem are called "theodicies."

One of the oldest theodicies was written by Plato in his dialogue *Timaeus*. He reasoned that "goodness," the creative or generative principle that underlies being, is so infinitely good that it creates every possible variety of thing—even bad things—in order to express the creative principle completely. This potent idea has been reiterated or else reinvented many times.

In the 1950s, a scientist named Hugh Everett III developed his "many-worlds interpretation" of quantum mechanics, a theory that took the immensely popular theme of "multiple universes"—a theme that can take many forms—in a distinctive direction that would generate a great deal of science fiction fantasy. The idea was that every single possibility—every conceivable kind of potentiality—must be actualized. And so the principle must play itself out through an infinite series of parallel dimensions or parallel universes.[2]

Every possible sequence of events must be happening *somewhere*. This is a convenient explanation of evil, and it rests upon the notion that the force behind everything is bound by a rigid kind of *logic*. God—or Fate—or Being—is forced by its nature to develop every single possibility. So there can be no blame for the evil that results; it is … destiny.

Paul Davies has explained the inspiration for this theory in the facts about quantum mechanics. As scientists conduct their observations, he explains, they will notice that at any given time a subatomic particle may lurch in one of two different possible directions—opposite directions—and no reason can be given for the path that the particle traverses.

He describes the situation in simplified terms as follows: the particle will "spin," he explains, but which way? Because of the uncertainty in quantum mechanics, we will never be able to predict the particle's direction. It may go "upward" or "downward" in its path, but we can never really know what will happen. For some mysterious reason, "there is an equal probability" for the particle to spin up or down.[3]

An "equal probability"—which implies that at the microscopic level our cosmos is wild, uncertain, and … "free."

Now watch the way in which this principle of quantum mechanics is applied to the "many-worlds" theory: at every instant when a "choice" between the two possibilities for particle "spin" has developed, "the universe splits into two copies, one in which the spin is up, the other in which it is down."[4]

Yes, the universe *splits into two copies*, so that *both* of the possibilities are actualized … in different universes.

Davies comes to the startling conclusion that this theory demands: "Everything that can happen, will happen." And this further implies (among a great many things) "there are stupendously many copies of ourselves in existence!"[5]

An engineer and science writer named Eugene Mallove once described the theory this way: "The universe continually bifurcates […] into a treelike infinity of parallel and disconnected worlds. All possible things happen 'somewhere.' In one universe, a cat dies, and in another it continues to live."[6]

This theory is a perfect theodicy: it implies that every single kind of evil is an absolute necessity.

A *necessity*. Now consider this interesting paradox: this theory, which began with *indeterminism*—specifically the fact that in quantum mechanics the behavior of subatomic particles is to some extent chaotic—leads straight to an iron-bound deterministic law. Take the propositions in sequence, one by one, and see where they lead: (1) no reason can be given for the particles to "spin" up or down. They just *do*. (2) Every possibility for spin *must be actualized*, which means that every possible or conceivable occurrence must be *acted out*. (3) *Therefore*, every single thing that can happen, *has to happen*—happen *somewhere*.

Creation would be "incomplete" if this principle did not hold good. And according to the theory, *creation simply has to be complete*.

More on that momentarily.

This notion was built into a more elaborate—and tragic—theological equivalent by Alfred North Whitehead in his book *Process and Reality*, which was published in 1929. He developed the idea that God is a "dipolar" being possessing two very different qualities: an unconscious side that is driven to create *every possible variety of thing*, and a conscious side that beholds all the evils that result from this creation and suffers—just as we suffer. Whitehead called God "the fellow sufferer who understands."[7]

Let us pause for a moment to notice something else about the vision of a "dipolar" God: one of the two poles is *active*. This is an interesting variation in the long and dominant tradition of monotheistic theology that avoids the many pitfalls in the traditional view that God is somehow "unchanging." The vision of a dipolar deity is one among many ideas in the tradition of "process theology," a movement that is grounded in the principle that God may indeed be evolving.

THE LIMITS OF LOGIC AS APPLIED TO METAPHYSICS

Back to the "many-worlds" theory. There are excellent reasons for finding this theory unpersuasive.

The most important of the reasons is this: the presupposition that when two possibilities develop, *both* of them have to be actualized is an exercise in merely *human* logic that may or may not be a *fantasy*. The unpleasant truth is that our versions of logic may sometimes be used to prove anything—or almost anything. Logical systems full of cleverness and elegance may easily be used (or misused) to "prove" completely opposite concepts.

One of the most engaging sections of Immanuel Kant's *Critique of Pure Reason* is called "The Antinomy of Pure Reason"—an "antinomy" being an incompatibility between two laws or *supposed* laws—and his method was to set forth opposite ideas (many of them cosmological) in two columns on the page, like this: (1) first column, "thesis: The world has a beginning in time, and is also limited as regards space"; (2) second column, "antithesis: The world has no beginning; and no limits in space; it is infinite as regards both time and space."[8]

Under each of these column headings—"thesis" and "antithesis"—he provides a logical … "proof."

Kant's exercise remains a salutary lesson in the fundamental limitations of "pure reason." The fact that our logic may lead us in a certain direction is no real protection from the possibility that we are fooling ourselves. Case in point: take the proposition that creation simply has to be "complete."

Oh, does it? Well, who says so? Can the proposition be proven? All right, *prove* it if you can, but the "proof" may be *no proof at all.*

Merely *human* suppositions may forever remain just that: human suppositions. And the logic that "proves" them may be nothing but an exercise in circular reasoning that leads right back to where it started: the suppositions.

Logic is important and at times indispensable, especially in light of the rant that we so often encounter in our interactions with others (especially in politics). And yet logic has its definite limits.

Consider a different example of a metaphysical theory that would seem to be consistent by the standards of its own internal logic but that leads upon full consideration to a dead-end—or worse.

Certain scientists and philosophers have embraced what some have called the concept of "block time," the concept that past, present, and future are nothing but fictitious categories in our minds and that "the present moment"— the ever-present *now*—is also a creation of our minds.

A key figure in this movement was the British philosopher J. M. E. McTaggart.

This belief that "eternity" (however one defines it) is the only true reality and that flux is *illusion* is rooted in themes of spirituality with ancient antecedents, not least of all the doctrines of Parmenides. In modern times, the idea has been embraced by some powerful philosophers. Kant came to the conclusion that "time is nothing but a form of inner sense," and that as to "objects as they may be in themselves, then time is nothing."[9] The same assertion was made even more emphatically by Schopenhauer.

In the twentieth century, an application of relativity theory to the structure of space-time gave the idea a new currency. The idea is to conceive of time as a dimension existing *all at once*, a kind of "spatialization" of time. In this view, the full extent of cosmic time *simply is*, which means that "the future" (if one can refer to such a thing with any cogency) already ... "is."

The mathematical physicist and philosopher Hermann Weyl once asserted that "the world does not happen, it simply is."[10] More recently, philosopher J. J. C. Smart has contended that "talk of the flow of time or the advance of consciousness is a dangerous metaphor that must not be taken literally."[11] Physicist David Park has stated that "one cannot perform any experiment to tell unambiguously whether time passes or not."[12]

Park may well be correct—there may be no way to settle the issue. There may be no way at all to prove that time passes and (conversely) no way to *disprove* it. No doubt the proponents of block-time theory feel the force of a certain kind of logic as they argue their points—but so do their opponents.

Philosopher Roberto Mangeira Unger and physicist Lee Smolin call time "the most real feature of the world." They proclaim that "everything changes [...] including change itself," and they insist that time really passes.[13]

So it goes: thesis and antithesis, thrust and parry, as the rival logicians duel it out. The block-time theorists contend that all appearances of change are "illusions"—*hallucinations*. Perhaps they are.

But have the block-time theorists developed a theory to *account for the fact* the universe seems to be in motion? Not really. Can they guide us—have they proposed any way for us to *act* if time is an illusion?

Not at all.

If block-time theory is true, then something else must be true, something else that can *account* for the fact that the reality we know is presented to us as a sequence of before and after. What is that something? The block-time theorists are stumped when it comes to that question. They are stumped because attempts to render time in the form of mere logic run afoul of two facts: (1) the mental powers we possess can never probe to the heart of ineffable things and

(2) the power of the words we concoct for the purpose of conducting our logical exercises may, if taken to the limit, peter out in mere fatuous word games.

And that means that all the people who tell us so complacently that our experience of past, present, and future is illusion are talking through their hats, talking nonsense: they do not have the faintest idea of what they mean.

Consider the example of a physicist named Julian Barbour who combined a version of block-time theory with the many-worlds theory in his sensation-causing 1999 book *The End of Time: The Next Revolution in Physics.*

The flow of time is an illusion, he wrote, though the presence of *now* is very real and it comprises every part of the universe. But in Barbour's conception there are infinite *nows* and they all exist simultaneously. They exist in an infinite realm that contains every possible *now*—every possible configuration that could constitute a universe—and he calls it Platonia.

Do these ideas sound suspiciously familiar?

The part of this theory that is never made sufficiently clear by Barbour—and that generates resistance—is his argument that time is illusory since every single *now* is self-contained. The encapsulization of *now* is complete, so there is no change at all in the static arrangements that comprise every possible cosmos. There *appears* to be change, for we are all deluded into feeling it.

The *now* that we "inhabit"—if the implications of Barbour's system can be trusted—has a "past" that never really existed. So the "memories" we think we possess are illusion. Indeed, our very continuity of selfhood (from moment to moment) is also illusion. We might as well be living in *The Matrix.*

And this leads to the obvious question: how can we be living a "life" without real *continuity?*

Barbour's theory makes no experiential sense, because it never explains what a static existence amounts to or how a static unit of ourselves can actually exist. *Now* as we know it is a *flow* that keeps slipping through our fingers as we *think* about it—*sequentially.* Experience is seamless.

However thin we try to slice our experience of *now*, it always *flows*—no one can disprove it.

Barbour has developed a logic that supports his theory, but a countervailing logic is out there. And so the old game of thesis and antithesis begins, and the predictable endgame is stalemate. He tells us that every *now* is frozen, and we answer back that *now* is organic. Who is right?

What is proven?[14]

Suppose for a moment that the *nows* we experience are something like the frames of a film. How do we account for the existence of this moving presentation—this "illusion?" We are dealing after all with a *sequence.*

What *is* it?

Barbour admits that his logic derives from an underlying presupposition. "I start," he proclaims, "from the philosophical conviction that the only true things are complete possible configurations of the universe, unchanging Nows."[15]

This "conviction"—as arbitrary as most other convictions that people assert dogmatically—is the basis for everything else in Barbour's theory. Others have the opposite conviction: Unger and Smolin, for example, who consider time "the most real feature of the world."[16]

It all comes down to the issue of sequence, which refutes all attempts to dismiss it.

How does Barbour account for our human experience of change? "The brain often fools us," he begins, and he suggests that our brains take "snap shots" and trick them out like a film. But listen to the way in which his language betrays him at once: "The brain processes information before we get it," he commences, having stumbled only five words into the sentence.[17]

Because he uses the fatal word "before."

The brain processes information *before we get it*, but what—pray tell—is the meaning of "before?"

Barbour's theory is a perfect illustration of the way in which logic can sometimes exceed its own limitations. It can lead us to embrace the sorts of notions that are *useless* in light of our experience.

Useless.

As William James once wrote, "the whole function of philosophy ought to be to find out what definite difference it will make to you and me, at definite instants of our life, if this world-formula or that world-formula be the true one."[18] "Difference" implies that things *can* be different and that *action* is a real possibility.

Both of the logical systems just described—the "many-worlds" theory and the "block-time" theory—could lead us into lives of passivity. They would make us feel essentially helpless. Consider: if all possible things must be happening *somewhere*, the lives we are leading are *predestined*. So why attempt to make anything different—what possible use could it do? It would be pointless.

And if *change* is an illusion, why attempt to do anything at all, since whatever you "do" is an *illusion*?

Meditation would appear to be the only real option that is left to us—except that mediation appears to be activity.

For those whose intuition obliges them to *trust* the authenticity of things that we feel can be different, a life of *action* is an absolute necessity. Are there spiritual justifications for insisting on a life of bold action?

THEORETICAL FREEDOM

It is time for us now to take a much closer look at "determinism:" the belief that things can *never* be in any way "different." According to determinism, everything has to be *just* the way it is, and it could never be anything else.

A scientific variation of this idea became standard a long time ago among "materialists." Their controlling idea was quite simple: linear causality within a Newtonian cosmos. They envisioned a simple chain reaction that emanates upward from subatomic particles to atoms to molecules to outward events that are forced to be just as they are through direct, straightforward, and implacable cause and effect.

But that worldview was altered over time by the impact of quantum mechanics, string theory, and a number of other speculations that have led great numbers of physicists to postulate a strange and paradoxical universe—one that refuses to behave by the standards of connect-the-dots logic.

If the constituent elements of reality revolve and pulsate together in 11-dimensional space (and also, perhaps, in some variety of multidimensional time), it is hard to believe any longer that the cosmos unfolds in a simple and linear pattern. To the contrary: the latest theories suggest a very open, contingent, spontaneous, and complicated universe.

In the middle of the twentieth century, some scientists examined the notions of multidimensional time that had been circulating for a great many years among laymen, some of them occultists. A British mathematician named John G. Bennett hypothesized in the 1950s and 1960s that some of these notions may be true. He reasoned that three different kinds of time may exist together: the succession of ever-changing "now" moments that we know, a structure to *contain* the succession (he called it "persistence"), and "hyparxis," a different time dimension that allows for *spontaneous change.*

The "elusive present," he wrote, which is "gone as soon as we reach it," is contained within a structural pattern—a channel of "persistence"—that encompasses the flow of events and *allows* it. And "hyparxis," the third time dimension, makes spontaneous change within the flow a possibility.

A "self-enabling" power is contained within this third time dimension that can *alter* the flow of events, make it *swerve*—and give us free will. Bennett called this the "power to connect or to disconnect the potential and the actual."[19]

Every possible sequence of events, he believed, may exist as a ghostly *potential*, and the endless possibilities, he said, are contained in a realm that he labeled "eternity." Most of them will never "come to life"—at least in *this* universe. But hyparxis makes the fate of every universe open-ended.

Three time dimensions—the now dimension, the channel dimension, and the crucial hyparxis dimension—three sides of the flow that is driving every universe, including our own, to its future.

Of course time could have far more dimensions than these; it might possibly compare to the 11-dimensional construction of string theory. Some argued in the twentieth century that time may have infinite dimensions. Heidegger wrote that "temporality" can manifest itself in different "ecstases," or outward projections, that may or may not be discernible in different "horizons," that is, presentational fields.[20]

In any case, there may clearly be *aspects* of time that are integral to our sense of volition: free will.

Free will: the spontaneous feeling that we have in the ever-present *now*, and this feeling is integral to everything we sense about existence. We sense that as the world is *becoming what it is*, there is a *freedom* at work that is combined with our own sense of *self*.

We sense that we are free—at least to some extent—and this feeling is integral to sanity. Our sanity, of course, is neither here nor there in the great scheme of things if our feeling of freedom is illusion.

Is it an illusion?

FREE WILL

Philosophers, theologians, and scientists have argued about this for ages. We *feel* volition, but philosophers in recent years have tended to be skeptics. Philosopher David Kyle Johnson spoke for many when he argued that even quantum physics has failed to establish free will.

While acknowledging that quantum events have "no cause"—and there is "more than one possible future"—he claimed that "this in no way saves free will." He continued: "Clearly, there are alternate possibilities in this scenario. But am I free? No, because the outcome of a quantum event is in no way up to me." We are, in his opinion, the outcome of random brain events.[21]

But this formulation has problems.

When Johnson employed the phrase "up to me," he glossed over the fact that what we know as our conscious self—what we think of as "me"—is deeply mysterious. Complex and organic, it seems to be more than just the sum of its parts: it is holistic. We can never pin it down, however unified it feels, and we do not understand how it works.

The role of quantum mechanics in the mental process remains a vexed question. No one knows how much freedom it gives, and no scientist has claimed that we have learned everything we need to learn about these secrets.

As Paul Davies has argued, "to claim that [...] brain activity renders free will an illusion is as misconceived as the claim that life is an illusion because of the underlying inanimate nature of atomic processes."[22]

This statement is convincing—except for the term "inanimate." Quantum physics suggests that atomic and subatomic processes are *"animate."*

"If body acts on mind, the reverse should also be true," in the opinion of Davies.[23] The cognitive scientist Douglas Hofstadter argues that consciousness *changes* the brain in what he calls a "Strange Loop" of reciprocity. If quantum events are antecedent to mental events, *this can work in reverse.*

The "observer principle" in quantum mechanics illustrates the point: an electron moves in what Davies calls a "hybrid" state until the gaze of an experimenter "forces the electron to make up its mind."[24]

This startling claim has been confirmed through experiments, though the usage "make up its mind" is an inference. These related theories will be probed in more detail by the end of the book.

Henry P. Stapp has explored the implications of quantum theory for the mind-brain-body continuum. He believes that quantum states possess an element of mind and this explains "how a person's mental intentions can affect that person's bodily actions in a way that he or she mentally intends."[25]

The result is a "model of the connection between mind and brain that is unlike anything previously imagined in science."[26]

Such ruminations seem hard for some contemporary philosophers to accept. But one philosopher who did embrace such a worldview was Alfred North Whitehead, who called the universe "organic."

The certitude of philosophers who dismiss free will is ill-grounded, for it rests upon *words.* We can go ahead and say that quantum events are "random"— words such as these can have their uses—but we can never know what a "random" event really ... *is.*

We are dealing here with secrets of nature, and philosophers—some of them—used to be more humble about acknowledging the limits of our powers. The things we observe give us no true knowledge of the hidden metaphysics *beyond,* in the opinion of David Hume. The "secret nature" of things, he suggested, "may change without any change in their sensible qualities."[27]

"It is easy to perceive what a darkness we are involved in," wrote John Locke. "We are so far from being admitted into the secrets of nature, that we scarce so much as ever approach the first entrance toward them." It is sobering, he wrote, to consider "how little it is of Being [...] that we are capable to know."[28]

Scientists continue to be haunted by this feeling, which was echoed by Sir James Jeans—a British physicist—in 1929: "It is difficult," he wrote, "to form even the remotest conception of the realities underlying all these phenomena. [...] They may be so fundamental as to be beyond the grasp of the human mind."[29]

To reiterate an earlier point: the logic and words at our disposal can never probe to the heart of ineffable things. The findings of quantum mechanics hint at "freedom" in the subatomic sphere, and we feel a volitional "freedom" in our daily activities that gives our decisions authenticity.

Are these illusions? Maybe. But they can neither be shrugged away nor disproven by the so-called logic of our limited minds. Discoveries of quantum physics were astonishing a century ago. Who can say what new discoveries await human beings in the centuries to come?

MIND

Our sense of self is a production of our minds. Our identity—our *being*—takes the form of awareness, and we wonder at times if this awareness is the product of our "physical" brains, and nothing more. Our minds in this view are productions of *matter*—the *matter* of the cosmos, the matter that is gathered in *us*.

Or perhaps it is the other way around.

Shift for a moment to the terms of ontology, and ask yourself this question: What is matter but a certain way of *being*? Philosophers and physicists have wondered for years about the relationship that obtains between the thing we think of as matter and the thing that we experience as mind.

There exists among the philosophers a long tradition of "pan-psychism"—the view that "matter" as we know it is composed by deeper force of *psychic energy*. Matter is indeed *reducible* to energy—according to the physicists.

The ancient Greeks had a term that was potent with future significance when they talked of the physical "stuff" of the cosmos and the way that it moves along in time: it was "*physis,*" the *way* things *behave*. The original concept of "*Tao*" in pre-Buddhist China was essentially the same.

Many of the pre-Socratics believed that the mysterious "physis" was *alive*.

Modern philosophic "Idealists"—those who believe that all reality is mentally based—have adopted different theories to apply their conviction that *mind* is antecedent to *things*. The presence of mind is an ongoing challenge to science. It implies a *precondition* that must flow from the nature of reality. Pan-psychists believe that this precondition is pervasive—in latent form.

Alfred North Whitehead developed a theory that within every "actual occasion" is psychic force. These occasions—which he also called "actual entities"—have physical and mental poles (like the dipolar God) and they explore each other through "prehensions."

Their psychic power may be latent and unconscious until a combination of them generates awareness—which is the case in our own minds and bodies.[30] But even in what seems to be the dull and inanimate universe, "mind" is on the move.

Many physicists have argued that the cosmos appears to have a built-in potential to "self-organize." It is more than coincidence, in the view of Paul Davies, that the universe generates greater complexity the longer it evolves, or that the universe is structured to support these patterns over very long periods of time, or that the patterns of complexity that generate life and awareness *cohere*—as in human DNA—instead of breaking apart into chaotic and random new patterns. There is "ingenuity" in nature, he muses, and our own existence and awareness cannot be accidental. He put it this way:

> I cannot believe that our existence in this universe is a mere quirk of fate. [...] Through conscious beings the universe has generated self-awareness. This can be no trivial detail, no minor byproduct of mindless, purposeless forces. We are truly meant to be here.[31]

There are "principles over and above the known laws of physics," he wrote. There are reasons why systems make "a sudden leap to a much more elaborate [...] state," as if they possess "*a will of their own*." There are laws "with an inbuilt facility for making interesting things happen"—laws that make the universe "free to create itself as it goes along." And these laws "have yet to be discovered."[32]

Life scientist Harold Morowitz argues that natural laws can create new laws through "emergence." He says that determinism is an oversimplification, observing that "the unfolding of the universe is not totally determined; neither is it totally random. The truth must lie somewhere in between."[33]

Psychiatrist and nature writer Paul R. Fleischman agrees that cosmic principles play out with "lawfulness and freedom, which do not contradict each other."[34] Put another way, the laws of physics are "channels that say 'yes,' 'no,' 'maybe,' 'sometimes,' 'never,' or 'later'" to the flow of events—guidelines that shape the course of emergence without determining the in-built freedom of the cosmos.[35]

In this view, the structure of the universe inherently generates novelty, accident, bursts of unpredictable creativity.

Do these theories of elemental *freedom* help us face the existence of evil—to confront the fact that our miraculous cosmos is generating many dreadful things? Are there implications for religion?

The answers to these questions are emotional as well as analytical. And yet our powers of analysis can help us to navigate the feelings.

FACING UP TO EVIL: HOW FREE IS THE UNIVERSE?

Conventional believers try to handle their reactions to evil in many different ways: through mysticism, through avoidance and denial, through belief in the fall of an earlier pristine existence—the destruction of Eden or some other earthly paradise—through belief in Satanic intervention, or belief in an all-compensatory afterlife.

Some think that "the Wisdom of the East" will give them hope in the face of desolation. So they seek it.

Many Buddhists suppress the inclination to attach much value to the transient pleasures of life, for they regard such things as illusions—"*maya*"—that deprive us of any real fulfillment. Serenity must come through transcendence—through the calming force of meditation.

Hence the calm resolution of the Buddhist monks who set fire to themselves in Vietnam to protest the persecution of Buddhists during the early 1960s. They were at peace through self-immolation.

Taoism offers the duality of Yin and Yang—the opposing but harmonious forces of nature. Meditation brings the calming realization that all supposed "opposites"—joy and horror, for example—make a "*Unity*" that constitutes the *Tao*. The trick is to mesmerize ourselves with this belief.

But such convictions are clearly not for everyone.

Some rebel: they may permit themselves—at least for a while—to "get angry at God" and his ways. Others conclude that an ethical life should be sufficient for a sane human being—that we have quite enough on our hands to account for our own thoughts and deeds without attempting to account for a world that we had no part in creating.

Some console themselves with the thought that God's workings are so far above our own that we can never understand them at all. Atheists have very different feelings.

But whenever we return to the question of "ontology"—Why does anything exist instead of nothing?—we come back to the mystery of being and its relationship to us.

Whatever force it may be that accounts for the cosmos and us—and there certainly seems to be force behind existence—is nothing that our minds can really fathom. And yet our own human nature was produced by its workings over eons. So what does that mean?

Two reciprocal ways of viewing the matter may be offered, in the form of two questions. Question one: What can the force of cosmic existence *mean to us* as we contemplate its workings? Question two: What can our lives *mean to it?* This latter question is not at all frivolous. Many believers have hoped down the years that our experience may *matter* in a way that goes far beyond our power to know and comprehend.

An ecumenical movement for "process theology" holds that our lives do matter to the force that created us and *help* that force in some way. The Jewish scholar Michael Lerner suggests that our welfare matters to God in a way that corresponds to the fact that the health of every cell within our body must matter to us. That may or may not be the case: it is an article of faith, or at least of conjecture.

Perhaps the best that we can do in our quest for an experience of natural religion is remind ourselves that our existence is after all a *gift*. We did not create ourselves; we were born, so our existence is "given." And we have the power to use our great gift to enhance life for others and ourselves.

Moreover, we can hope—or pray—that by the use of this power we contribute to something that is "higher."

When we feel an exhilarating "rush" now and then—in our moments of triumph—we experience *spontaneous power*. Determinists say that this experience is nothing but illusion. If all possible things must be happening *somewhere*, our lives are just a matter of *fate* and our power is *reflex*.

But we sense that this is very unlikely.

For the notion is simply too tidy a construction of our own human reasoning and logic. The force behind everything, the force that we can feel every moment of our lives, is *not* human, so applying the patterns of our own human logic to its workings is obviously folly. Consider an example.

We can easily conceive—if we follow the promptings of our logic—of an infinite state of "unbeing." We can easily persuade ourselves that nothing really has to exist. As Davies has affirmed, "one can certainly imagine that neither God nor the universe existed," and "there does not seem to be any logical contradiction" in the statement.[36]

One of the cardinal tenets of monotheistic religion is the proposition that God "always" existed. But one could surely argue that according to a *certain* kind of logic such a proposition is ... "illogical." After all, it *stands to reason* that, according to a *certain kind of logic*, everything must have a *cause*. God *doesn't* have a cause—if the standard doctrine is correct—he simply *is*.

Alfred North Whitehead once reflected that the very existence of God is "the ultimate irrationality."[37]

And this relates to his remarkable statement that religion is a way to account for the fact that "what cannot be, yet is." What "*cannot be*"—at least by the standards of a certain kind of logic—yet *is*.

This striking proposition can lead us to some liberating types of conclusions.

The fact that anything exists suggests a wild sort of freedom that cannot be explained by human logic. The ever-present *now* is a fact that we can never understand. It is "given." But what "gives" it?

Something greater by far than any theory that our minds can conceive, something *free* to be just what it is. Nothing *has to* exist by the standards of our logic, but the fact that things *do* shows that being and freedom *go together*. Perhaps being and freedom are *dimensions* of a much greater power.

Let us pause to consider the conceptual breakthrough that gave the world quantum mechanics: the experiments were treated as *action*, right down to the behavior of the subatomic quanta.

And the result was revolutionary.

Henry Stapp sums it up this way: "the aspects of nature represented by the theory are converted from elements of *being* to elements of *doing*." Instead of a "world of *material substances*," we were given a world that is inherently dynamic, a world that is "populated by *actions*."[38]

What does this radical shift in the worldview of scientists mean as we contemplate the cosmos?

It is easy enough to conclude that such issues are beyond us—and give up the quest. Yet a "dance" is going on all around us and within us and its pulses are gathered into structures, including ourselves.

We were *given* a chance to make our own contributions to creation. Shall we make the most of it?

CHAPTER 4

FREEDOM, SPIRITUALITY,
AND STRUGGLE

What kind of a universe is this—what kind of a world do we inhabit? If a wild sort of freedom is implied by existence, how exactly does the universe work? We see a great many objects that appear to be anything but "free."

We feel a *limited* freedom in ourselves—a mental volition that is capable of choices. Yet our bodily functions are largely automatic and the thought that any nonorganic objects have "freedom" would seem to be absurd.

Yet the school of philosophy known as pan-psychism may someday prove to have merit. Psychic force may be latent in everything, and this notion has a very long lineage in philosophic thinking. The following philosophers flirted with the theory to one extent or another: Heraclitus, Leibniz, Hegel, Schopenhauer, Bergson, James, and Whitehead, among many others. The foremost contemporary advocate is the philosopher David Chalmers. The theologian Pierre Teilhard de Chardin also embraced it.

The theory has many variations, but Whitehead's variation is in certain ways the strongest.

It holds that the tiniest pulses of existence are imbued with a miniscule dose of *sense*—it is not necessarily conscious—that will ramify "upward" into patterns of puissance and power. The aggregations may appear to us static (inert) or dynamic, depending upon the specific convergence that creates them. Some will reach a *critical mass* that imbues the results with *awareness* and consciousness of *will*.

Could this theory be true? Who can say?

But Whitehead composed a suggestive passage to *express* this theory in relation to human sensibilities. He describes the way in which our mental process partakes of a flow that is greater than ourselves. Every moment, he wrote, we experience a sense of emotional feeling, belonging to oneself in the past, passing into oneself in the present, and passing from oneself in the present towards oneself in the future; a sense of influx of influence from other vaguer presences in the past, localized and yet evading local definition, such influences modifying, enhancing, inhibiting, diverting, the stream of feeling which we are receiving, unifying, enjoying, and transmitting.[1]

This is our place in the dance of "prehensions" that are pulsing through the process of time.

A very different application of the concept—or something akin to it—was developed by Arthur Schopenhauer. He contended that "Will" is the force behind existence. But this version of pan-psychism was deeply pessimistic.

"Will" in the system of Schopenhauer is nothing but blind *appetite*—a source of "mind" that is *mindless*. Rather than submit to being such a creature, Schopenhauer turned to the side of Buddhism and Hinduism that views the visible and sensible reality around us as insubstantial or in some sense illusory.

In the unforgettable conclusion to his magnum opus, *The World as Will and Representation*, the philosopher bade us renounce the force of will and seek tranquility in … nothing. And he meant that particular admonition to be taken as literally as possible. "We freely acknowledge," he wrote, "that what remains after the complete abolition of the will is, for all who are still full of will, assuredly nothing. But also conversely, to those in whom the will has turned and denied itself, this very real world of ours with all its suns and galaxies, is—nothing."[2]

The contradictions are obvious enough, and this formula necessitates behavior close to self-hypnosis. Schopenhauer himself—a man full or spirit, astringent wit, and keen argumentation—found it hard to live up to this ideal, if one can call it an ideal.

The philosopher Arthur O. Lovejoy once wrote that this particular strain of otherworldly and mystical thought discloses "the strange truth that many of the great philosophers and theologians have been occupied with teaching the worship of—nonentity; though of nonentity made to seem more 'real' and emotionally more satisfying by an emphasis on its freedom from the particular defects and limitations […] which characterize all the concrete objects of which we can think at all."[3]

Most of the applications of pan-psychism have been far from doctrines of "nonentity." To the contrary—they embrace a reality imbued with dynamism, an existence to be lived through—by those who are alive—with vigor. But this existence can lead to brutal pain as well as fulfillment.

DEVASTATION AND HUMAN SENSIBILITIES

Based upon this kind of speculation, a theological theory may be offered that does justice to a great many things.

Many people understandably wish to believe in a supernatural being who protects us. But then—if they can free themselves for a while from the doctrines that were force-fed to them as children—they take a candid look at the world and find it distressing. True, they can marvel at the mystery of being—if they take just a moment to *think*—and be grateful for awareness and identity. But when they think of all the savagery and pain in the cosmos, their mood begins to darken.

They think about carnivorism and sadism and psychopathology. They reflect upon the fact that every living thing must sustain itself by *devouring* what used to be the substance of other living things, and their mood becomes darker still.

They find that their faith in a benevolent and merciful deity is shaken to the point where they fall back upon the power (such as it is) of *blind faith*— or they seek to find release through a gesture of prayer—in order to sustain themselves as they contemplate what the novelist Graham Greene once called "the appalling strangeness of the mercy of God."

But another path remains open to them—a path that can lead them to a very different spirituality, one that may be said to be stronger, better grounded, and more tough-minded than others. This alternative spirituality appreciates the miracle of life but it also protects us from the wishful thinking and false sentimentality—the double-talk that some religions dispense as they attempt to palliate the horror that we see in the world.

Let us explore this variation in spirituality as *theory*.

Begin with a *conclusion*: whatever force is responsible for *being-as-such* is ineffable to us. The acknowledgement of this is a sine qua non if we wish to get rid of superstition. Let it take the form of a *confession*: we *confess* to ourselves that we have no idea of what the force behind existence might be. It would surely be *pleasant* for us (to put it mildly) to *know* what God is, but we need to face a truth that no amount of mumbo jumbo can displace: our theories and our mystic "revelations" can never give us *knowledge* of ultimate realities. Oracles can share the results of their trances to their hearts' content—they can do it all they wish—but they can never *prove* a single thing they say.

There is clearly a force behind existence, but we have no idea of what it is. Its nature and its workings are completely *concealed* from us.

We can, however, reach a tentative and important conclusion about this force: it seems to have a *freedom* that defies our human logic. We can play the mental game of imagining "nothing," so the fact that things *exist* implies a "sovereignty" for which no human reason can be given.

This *freedom*—this "sovereignty"—in some manner we can never understand seems to "throw" the universal process into development. Cosmic emanations are *propelled*—or so it would appear. Heidegger used the term "thrown" to describe the condition of "being-ness" that is inherent in the human condition (as we experience it), and perhaps it is defensible here to apply this term to the cosmos as a whole.

Heidegger's metaphor was captivating, so it bears a brief explanation. He said that we are "thrown" and "falling," by which he meant that the human experience of "being-ness" (he called it "Dasein," which in German means being-*there*) is equivalent to an object hurtling through space; in our experience of being-in-motion we were *launched* into the world via birth and our trajectory of life will bring us "downward" to the outcome of death.[4]

Some physicists believe that the universe is traversing a comparable arc, which lasts for eons; the dynamism that emerged from the "Bang" will perhaps "burn out" over time, or contract, to form the basis for yet another "Bang."

The metaphor that equates our lives to the trajectories of hurtling objects conveys a sense of passivity—even helplessness—and it could lead us into determinism if we let it. But we are *not* really helpless or passive—we are *active* to a very great extent. Determinists deny it, but we feel it every moment of our lives. As we "hurtle" along, we are capable of *doing* many things that may alter the vectors of the world.

The findings of quantum mechanics—confirmed through mathematics— seem to bear it out.

WILD FREEDOM—OR MORAL CHAOS?

The findings of quantum mechanics were enhanced in recent decades by the advent of string theory. Both of these inquiries suggest that a mysterious reality exists at the subatomic level, one that is imbued with indeterminacy—a radical and perhaps inherent uncertainty. The question of how this indeterminacy affects the morphology of things at the macrocosmic level is complicated.

Recall that observations have shown that when two possible paths have developed for a particle, nothing can predict the way it goes. Laboratory experiments have been conducted to study this problem. The results in one case, according to Paul Davies, suggest the possibility that an "overlap of phantom alternatives" is always in play, and that "the worlds of path 1 and path 2 are superimposed on each other to form a hybrid reality."[5]

A hybrid reality? Or perhaps it would be better to call it an overlapping of simultaneous chances, *both* of which may be simultaneously coming true—*or not*. Is that strange enough? No, for this theory gets stranger still. Two sets of photons (a beam of laser light was divided and then subdivided through some crystals and mirrors) were passed through detectors. When the scientists studied the results, they found that their *observation* seemed to *change* the results—somehow.

The details of the experiment were complicated, and most of them need not detain us. But the gist of it came down to this: two sets of photons (dubbed "signal photons" and "idler photons" were set in motion. When the scientists tried to track the "signal photons," the results were fuzzy. But as soon as they tried to track the "idler photons," the paths of the other ones were clear. "Without actually *doing* anything directly to the signal photons," Davies observed, "the experimenters found that the signal photons adjusted their behavior." It was as if the two sets of photons were communicating, as if they "are psychic."[6]

Psychic.

Please note that the term was applied to this particular situation by a *scientist*—not a layman.

"Quantum cosmologists" continue to probe into the "general quantum state" of the universe. They struggle to understand what Davies calls the "timeless quantum frolic" that appears to be lurking in outward events, notwithstanding their appearances of regularity and order.[7]

Many have taken the findings of quantum mechanics to imply that within the propulsion of the cosmos, there seems to be ... "hyparxis." The theological application is striking: it would seem as though the freedom represented by existence itself may extend—via microcosmic patterns—*in* existence. The theory of pan-psychism obviously adds to these sorts of speculations. In other words, the freedom that accounts for the universe may be *contained in the fabric* of the universe.

The universe apparently erupted from the cosmic "singularity"—this is the consensus of opinion these days among a great many physicists—and (unless the determinists are right) this universe is actively "self-organizing."

It appears that the spontaneity of action at the subatomic level keeps this process moving ceaselessly on. And the patterns of cosmic evolution spread out into vast aggregations of complexity that last for eons.

We know perfectly well that we constitute *one* variety of power aggregation in the universe—among many others. The quantum creativity of subatomic action will generate endless kinds of things. At times they exist in symbiosis, but they sometimes *collide* with each other and *destroy* each other and *feed upon* each other: it is "in their nature" to do so.

It is simply "the way that things are."

Is this not a fair description of the way in which the universe seems to function—according to the best sense-data that our minds have been able to gather?

It is time to apply these propositions—some of them speculative—to a theological proposition that is totally speculative. Let us frame it in terms of the monotheistic tradition for reasons of convenience.

In general terms we may envision the cosmos as an emanation from a source—an emanation imbued with an element of freedom and supported by the ever-present *now*. The *power* of God may be said to be *immanent* in his cosmos, but he does not appear to "take sides" in any situations. The idea that God intervenes now and then to reward or to punish or protect can never be proven.

It is best, therefore, to presume that no divine intervention in specific events is occurring: we are "on our own" in this respect.

In the eighteenth century, there used to be a term for this particular type of theological construction: it was called "deism." The idea was straightforward and simple enough: God set the universe in motion and it runs forever on its own. People like Thomas Jefferson—participants in the Enlightenment—were deists.

There is much to be said for this particular theory if we seek to explain the world around us. The universe may be justly imagined as an open-ended process—a free-for-all in which entities surge unimpeded by the guidance or the moral direction of a gray-bearded father in heaven.

In emotional terms, this pattern of belief is a double-sided thing. On the positive side, it allows us *without superstition* to experience the beauty and the glory of existence. It allows us *without superstition* to glory in the fact that we are granted a miraculous *day* before we lapse into … night.

That is surely an experience that every single one of us deserves to have at some time. And the deists let us have it unspoiled—unsullied by the orthodoxies and the dogmas of other people. We have the pleasure of enjoying it "neat."

And yet the deist creed by itself is insufficient in a fundamental way: it does us little good if we are forced to come to grips in emotional terms with the somber underside of existence—with the problem of evil.

For we live in a universe that manifests itself in half-orderly and half-chaotic ways.

We are living an adventure that is thrilling but disturbing since the world both supports us and threatens us. We are *embattled* as we struggle for serenity.

We must struggle to protect what is our own.

RESCUE

We see the innocent torn limb from limb, we see the loathsome and incurable diseases ruin lives, and then we wonder, as anyone with sense always does: is the spontaneity of creation nothing better than chaos?

There are times when that seems to be the case.

But there is often consolation for us in the power we possess within ourselves. Heartbreak may ravage us, and yet *resilience* can overcome sorrow. If we resolve we will never be defeated, we can take the old instincts and shape them anew into a venture that will make the world better.

The very fact that we constitute a species with moral sensibilities is telling. For as we brace ourselves to the darker realities and brave the tragic challenges of life—as we summon the strength that we possess to perform what we feel to be our duty—we are acting in a spiritual way.

After all: our sense of decency *like everything else* is an emanation from the force behind the universe. How else could it have possibly arisen? It relates in some way—this point has to follow—with *potentialities* that had to be latent in the force behind us all: the force that some people call God.

Like everything else within the great free-for-all of existence, we are acting in accordance with our nature. But it just so happens that our nature includes the force of conscience. We can choose to show decency and we can also experience love within the limits that the cosmos permits. And when we encounter cruelty—whether in the actions of others or even in ourselves— we can summon the impulse of love and then *shape* it as a force that can protect.

A crucial caveat, this: for in order to act upon the impulse of love, we must sometimes use it to *protect*. And in order to *protect*, we must sometimes *destroy* the threats of harm—whether they derive from human action or not.

We must arise and do battle with some other parts of the universe.

Perhaps in doing these things we are giving something relatively new to our corner of the cosmos. And if so—this point has been made by so many great teachers down the years—then our gesture is worth it. We are capable, at least to a limited extent, of what the Hebrews of old called *Tikkun Olam*: the duty to strive all we can to effectuate "repair of the world."

And is this what "the good Lord intends"? The question of course is unanswerable, and yet it leads us to an issue that no one who is decent or sane should try to avoid: the issue of responsibility.

The form that this universe possesses is not of our making: whatever guilt we may happen to incur in our lives, we are not the creators of the universe. We are surely not to blame for what it is. And yet our sanity commands us to scrutinize its workings and judge them if they threaten our values.

If we wish to "blame God" for the fact that the universe happens to be what it is, so be it, except for this proviso: without question—without any question at all—we believe it is right for the universe and life to be here, and that compared to the hypothesis of endless nothingness, being and existence are *right*.

We believe such things—unless we are nihilists, or worshippers of death, or psychopaths.

We are glad to be here—thankful for the very fact of *being*. And perhaps this is creed enough for those who have the wit to embrace it, so long as we are mindful of the ethical imperative.

Some would call this creed "existentialism," but the term is too encumbered with baggage. "Pragmatism" might apply to some of its tenets (William James would probably agree). But feel free to call it anything you wish to … if you want it.

A creed such as this one has no need for myths—or dogmas or lies. A religious creed such as this one is based upon truths—or call them strong human values if you wish—that are real.

Real enough for the people among us who insist upon thinking for themselves. This is *one* potential form of spirituality for independent people.

And there are others.

CHAPTER 5

THEOLOGY AND WORSHIP

Which comes first: theology or worship?

Either one can influence the other: our emotional need to engage in worship may prompt the creation of theology. But this process can easily run in the reverse when theology dictates worship. Free thinkers may begin at either end of this open continuum. The case can be made that nondogmatic spirituality may be formed in accordance with heterodox *instincts*—instincts that can lead to diverse theological constructions.

William James made some telling observations about such alternative forms of spirituality. He indulged the idea, for example, of renewed applications of polytheism, observing that belief in many gods—people often worship many gods without knowing it—"has always been the real religion of common people, and is so still today."[1]

Roman Catholicism provides a convenient example of this tendency to have one's cake and eat it in theological terms, for within an overall rubric of "monotheism"—the worship of *one God*—one can also selectively worship God the father, Jesus, Mary, the members of the angelic hierarchy, and the saints. Catholics interact with a large pantheon of supernatural of semi-supernatural beings.

Would a more directly and *frankly* polytheistic approach to spirituality be possible in this day and age? There are, of course, existing polytheistic systems widely in use—Hinduism, for example—but what about the creation of new ones?

POLYTHEISM CONSIDERED

James developed something of a formula for the cultivation of this idea. He suggested that the simplest form of spirituality was perhaps

45

the belief that beyond each man and in a fashion continuous with him there exists a larger power which is friendly to him and to his ideals. All that the facts require is that the power should be both other and larger than our conscious selves. Anything larger will do, if only it be large enough to trust for the next step. It need not be infinite, it need not be solitary.

And he argued that "a final philosophy of religion will have to consider the pluralistic hypothesis more seriously than it has hitherto been willing to consider it."[2]

It is engaging, even entertaining, to consider this possibility. The ancient polytheistic systems give plenty of precedent. Would it not be cheerful, in our own here and now, to select a Greek Olympian as one's very own personal champion—to glory, for instance, in a bond with the goddess Athena, to tell one's self that this superb armed maiden, full of wisdom—Athena *Promachos*, Athena *Parthenos*—is available for help and protection? The possibilities were demonstrated (vicariously) years ago when translator Dudley Fitts rendered this joyous chorus from an Aristophanes play in modern English:

> I dance in the name
>
> Of Apollo: O Music!
>
> I dance in the name
>
> Of Artemis: chaste Archer!
>
> > Defense from afar!
>
> I dance in the name
>
> Of Hera: Bride Goddess![3]

And so on.

But in serious terms, attempts to develop this idea as the basis for a *new* form of spirituality would perforce be exercises in light-hearted fantasy—as the facts of everyday life would demonstrate. And probing deeper, one might gradually recall that the polytheistic systems of ancient times were grounded in a *unitary* mystery that could be rendered in monotheistic or at least monistic terms.

Hesiod, who apparently lived between the seventh and eighth centuries BC, told in his *Theogony* of how generations of supernatural beings—monsters, giants, gorgons, furies, titans, and Olympian gods—evolved through the sex-like interaction of primal entities such as earth and heaven. But these successive generations of deities and supernatural beings emerged from a primal *unitary* source, namely, the "Chasm."

Similarly, the long-lived and surviving polytheistic system of Hinduism is grounded in a principle that might well be regarded as monotheistic or more accurately pantheistic: "Brahman," the reality from which the divinities like Shiva and Vishnu and all the "avatars" derive.

So the supposed existence of "lesser" deities begs the question of what underlying principle accounts for reality itself.

Hinduism is an interesting case in point, for there are positive values in this belief system. A significant degree of flexibility is present in the Hindu tradition, which has generated works of great subtlety, especially the Upanishads. And even on the humdrum level, cult devotions of innumerable deities that millions of Hindus observe every day are in many respects quite harmless.

Even so, like any religion, the Hindu tradition has a darker side that can generate abuse. Hinduism is perforce complicit in the infamous caste system, and "Hindu Nationalism" can oppress. There are always complaints within Hindu culture from the free-thinking people who chafe at being told what to wear, what to eat—what to think. A prominent example is the Indian philosopher Meera Nanda, whose manifesto for secular enlightenment bears the following title: *Prophets Facing Backwards: Postmodern Critiques of Science and Hindu Nationalism in India.*

Any attempts to create new polytheistic belief systems run afoul of the fact that they involve new myth-making, and myths (alas) seem to lead more or less irrevocably to new dogmas. Or worse: as a cautionary tale, we need only remember how some of the Nazis attempted to resurrect belief in the old Norse gods as they developed their sick and revolting new pagan religion—with its ritual of human sacrifice. And some of them believed in a sun god: a deity of "blondeness."[4]

Dare we take the risk of taking up William James on his suggestion? The question must remain open-ended.

DUALISM CONSIDERED

The impulse to conceive of a twofold division of supernatural force—commonly rendered as a struggle between "good and evil"—could also be labeled "the real religion of common people" to some extent.

Dualistic religion can just as dangerous in its way as polytheistic religion or monotheistic religion—just as liable to abuse.

Here's an example: the tendency to conceive of *physicality* as "evil" when compared to the "purity" of disembodied "spirit." This was the basis of the ancient Persian religion, "Mazdaism"—a religion successively expressed in the forms of "Zoroastrianism" and "Manichaeism." According to this tradition, emanations from the good deity Ahura Mazda (pure spirit), were imprisoned by the evil spirit Ahriman in gross matter—and gross flesh. Consequently, the pure spirit that resides within us all is constantly struggling to return to its primal source.

This powerful notion led to various forms of asceticism and self-denial in Western culture. It infiltrated the culture of ancient Greece, for example, and Plato made use of it when he distinguished between the "higher" realm of pure "Ideas" and the *lower* realm of transience. He went further: in many of his writings, he expressed the belief that an emphasis on pleasure and carnality was a hindrance to the soul as it sought to uplift itself. In *Phaedo*, he went so far as to put this point of view into the mouth of Socrates, who tells some friends who are visiting him in prison that he is *eager* to drink the poison hemlock, thus escaping from the prison of flesh.

The notion also infiltrated Gnosticism, an early Christian heresy in which God the father (and here is the heresy) was sometimes regarded as an *evil* deity—one whose act of Genesis *imprisoned* pure spirit in the incarnation of matter. Jesus, conversely, is a glorious rebel who can help the soul escape from the prison that Jehovah created to torture us.

Willy-nilly, the notion crept forward in orthodox Catholicism via the doctrine of celibacy as a pathway to holiness. It gained particular force in the imputation of original sin to sexuality. For many of us, the pernicious consequences of this dualism are obvious in the repressions of Eros that afflict the believers who regard the experience of sexuality with ludicrous guilt.

Take a more generalized example of the dangers of dualism. "Evil" is sometimes—not always, but sometimes—a hard quality to define. We regard malevolent opponents as evil, but what if we believe that we may have to use their own tactics against them in order to defeat them? Is it necessarily evil to treat some rough customers in rough ways? Is it always hypocritical to "fight fire with fire?"

Sincere, conscientious, and ethical people will often disagree about these matters.

The theologian Reinhold Niebuhr once observed that the self-styled "children of light" must sometimes *learn* from the putative "children of darkness" without becoming *like them*. This complicates the problem of evil, since ambiguity is sometimes inextricable from moral challenges. Dualism taken to extremes may oversimplify morality and lead to a perfectionism that plays into the hands of predation. This happens whenever conscientious people succumb to the notion that they and people like them must never—ever—"dirty their hands."

Such beliefs are demonstrably utopian—impossible for people with strategic minds to entertain. An excessive *separation* of "goodness" from "evil" may also lead us to demonize opponents in a way that can boomerang.

On the other hand, some opponents—like Nazis—are so *close to* "demonic" that we might as well *regard* them as demonic—metaphorically speaking.

Niebuhr put the matter in mildly rationalistic terms when he observed that "the children of light are foolish not merely because they underestimate the power of self-interest among the children of darkness. They underestimate the power among themselves."[5]

This insight is fundamentally *Taoist.* The Chinese sage Chuang Tzu (or Zhuang Zhou) put the matter this way in the third century BC:

> The sayings, "Shall we not follow and honour the right and have nothing to do with the wrong?" and "Shall we not follow and honour those who secure good government and have nothing to do with those who produce disorder?" show a want of acquaintance with the principles of Heaven and Earth; it is like following Heaven and taking no account of Earth; it is like following and honouring the *yin* and taking no account of the *yang*.[6]

There is another form of dualism that takes some of these problems in rather pessimistic directions: the impulse to envision a war between the force of "being" (good) and the dialectically opposite (and therefore evil) force of "unbeing." Dylan Thomas's admonition to "rage, rage against the dying of the light" can serve as a hymn for this particular application of spirituality.

This dualism can be found in the work of Sigmund Freud, who envisioned a cosmic struggle between "Eros," the creative universal life force, and a "death instinct" that seeks to destroy whatever Eros creates. Later Freudians called this the duality of "Eros and Thanatos."

In this dialectical separation of "being" from aggressive "unbeing," the phenomenon of "becoming"—the *synthesis* of this cosmic tug of war—becomes tragic. Freud, in his book *Civilization and Its Discontents*, adopted this view in regard to the human predicament. One possible response to such a tragic view of the human predicament is fatalism. Hence the faith tradition that *accepts* death and loss with serenity—that *surrenders* itself to the reality that "nothing can last."

There is also, however, a tradition that *welcomes* "becoming," with its novelty and change. Arthur O. Lovejoy commented once on belief systems that are centered in visions of an afterlife that is beautiful because it is *exciting*. A great many people, he wrote, "find something very solid and engrossing" in dynamic change. He invoked the "breezy gusto" of Robert Browning, who, in his poem *Epilogue*, bade us "greet the unseen with a cheer, crying 'speed—fight on, fare ever, there as here.'"

This particular believer finds "comfort in some vision of a better 'this world' to come, in which no desire should lack fulfillment and his own zest for things should be permanently revitalized."[7]

Yet another iteration of dualism ought to be considered, though its precepts are surely "not for everyone." One of the most interesting ventures in developing a dualistic spirituality was the system of Georg Wilhelm Friedrich Hegel, as introduced in his seminal work, *Phenomenology of Spirit* (1807). In simplified terms, Hegel's surrogate for God—the Absolute—is creative, reaching out eternally to a realm that is distinct from itself—that is, "nature."

The Absolute possesses the attributes of "self," whereas nature begins as "un-self." The Absolute generates nature and proceeds to interact with it. It returns to itself and then proceeds to venture forth again in a cyclical pattern that is playing out every moment *instantly*. The endless and constant interaction between these two dialectical poles creates "the world" that we know and experience.

The same concept was integral in certain respects to the Hindu cosmology: the Absolute—Brahman—becomes the world and then returns to itself. The god Krishna describes the rhythmic ebb and flow in the Bhagavad Gita: "At the end of the night of time all things return to my nature; and when the new day of time begins I bring them again into light. Thus through my nature I bring forth all creation and this rolls around in the circles of time."[8] The idea is so simple it has doubtless occurred to any number of people as they think about religion. But Hegel used it as the basis for imputing dialectics to the innermost fabric of nature.

Hegel was at times a turgid writer, so perhaps it would be best to explicate his system in the words of someone else. We will use a description composed by Martin Heidegger, who offered a sketch of Hegelian dialectics as applied to the existence of "space." Yet be warned: Heidegger's rendering of Hegel's ideas is not much of an improvement over Hegel's original prose.

Here is what Heidegger wrote (in English translation, of course): "The point, in so far as it differentiates anything in space, is the *negation* of space, though in such a manner that, as this negation, in itself remains in space; a point is space after all."[9] In other words, a "point" is a reification of the "self/not-self" dialectic in spatial terms.

Thus a point is both a part of space *and yet not a part of space* in this exercise.

Then, as every point engages in this "self/not-self" dialectic, it will generate time, or a temporal dimension. Here is the general idea (brace yourself for this):

> In the negation of negation (that is, of punctuality) the point posits itself *for itself* and thus emerges from the indifference of subsisting. As that which is posited for itself, it differentiates itself from this one and that one: it is *no longer* this and *not yet* that. In positing itself for itself, it posits the succession in which it stands—the sphere of Being-outside-of-itself, which is by now the sphere of negated negation. [...] According to Hegel, this negation of the negation as punctuality is time.[10]

In other words, the pulsations of "points" within the ever-flickering plenum of space create another dimension—time.

One of the interesting things about this whole formulation is the way it anticipates the discovery of "space-time"—the fabric in which spatiality and temporality are interwoven—a hundred years later. It also anticipates some aspects of quantum mechanics.

Can the abstract formulations of Hegel serve anyone's emotional needs? The question borders on a joke. Those with a mathematical bent might relate to this version of dualism, since Hegelian logic is in some ways close to mathematical thinking. But others have made the same principles far more accessible. "Hegelian dialectics" are a latter-day rendering of ideas that have been used many times by many people: ideas that derive from the perennial impulse to break things down into opposite principles that lend themselves to reconciliation through a process of *synthesis*.

Such has been the message of Taoism through the ages. The harmonizing of Yin and Yang through *balance* has been offered by innumerable Chinese sages as the surest path to wisdom.

VARIATIONS OF MONOTHEISM CONSIDERED

Monotheism—the creed that embraces only one divine force—may be subdivided in ways that partake of duality.

Take its application as "theism": the creed that insists upon distinguishing "the creator" from the metaphysically distinct *creation* that should not be confused with its source. In theistic systems, the creative force and the resulting creation are *not the same thing*, so the result is an obvious duality.

"Pantheism," the creed that views God as encompassing *everything*, has a kind of duality as well. There is a "monist" side to the pantheist tradition—as represented in Spinoza's philosophy—a worldview that emphasizes the single, holistic, and unified *totality* of everything. But "everything" in the universe as we know it manifests itself as an obvious *plurality*. And so pantheists like the naturalist John Muir have gone out of their way to emphasize the many different forms in which spirit can appear. And they have done so with joyous abandon. Consequently, the pantheist outlook may be said to have distinct monistic and pluralistic "sides" and the implications for worship differ accordingly.

The monistic side of pantheism can be applied to the experience of worship through meditation. The practices of meditation or "mindfulness" coax the mind into a state in which a *bond* between consciousness and the *unity* of all existence takes over. The result can be peaceful or blissful euphoria that those who have experienced it have sometimes called a "forgetfulness of self."

The benefits of such serenity in psychological and spiritual terms are obvious. There is nonetheless a price to be paid: a sacrifice of independent thinking and *feeling* if the practice is taken too far. Anyone who treasures their power to think for themselves or experience the *joys of living* must reflect long and hard about the precept—particularly strong in certain schools of Buddhism—that the object of meditation is to *banish* such things: to *silence* conscious thought and *repress* our sense of individual selfhood and everyday pleasure.

Those who believe in an independent spirituality must consider the meditational method merely an occasional—rather than a constant—opportunity for peace if they value independence.

Fortunately, "Eastern wisdom" provides a more enticing option than the disciplined renunciation of a Buddhist monk. The old Chinese emphasis on the need for *variation* in human moods and needs—derived from the *dualist* interplay of Yin and Yang within the one single *unity* of *Tao*—offers a healthier and better-rounded option for independent people. The interplay between the other-worldliness of Taoism and the worldliness of Confucianism is exemplified in the teachings of the twelfth-century sage Zhu Xi, or Chu Hsi, who preached a life of intelligent, reflective, and spiritual *action*.

Here, if anywhere, is an application of spirituality that lends itself to the exuberant side of *living*.

A *dynamic* euphoria—not based in tranquility but rather in the *thrill* and *stimulation* of existence—represents an alternative spirituality that links the monistic and pluralistic realms. An illustration may be found within the writings of James Joyce, specifically the passage in *Portrait of the Artist as a Young Man* in which Stephen Dedalus is seized by a powerful epiphany. An extended quotation is in order, and the words that follow are—fortunately—in the public domain:

> Now, as never before, his strange name seemed to him a prophecy. So timeless seemed the grey warm air, so fluid and impersonal his own mood, that all ages were as one to him. A moment before the ghost of the ancient kingdom of the Danes had looked forth through the vesture of the haze-wrapped city. Now, at the name of the fabulous artificer, he seemed to hear the noise of dim waves and to see a winged form flying above the waves and slowly climbing the air. What did it mean? Was it a quaint device opening a page of some medieval book of prophecies and symbols, a hawklike man flying sunward above the sea, a prophecy of the end had been born to serve and had been following through the mists of childhood and boyhood, a symbol of the artist forging anew in his workshop out of the sluggish matter of the earth a new soaring impalpable imperishable being?

> His heart trembled; his breath came faster and a wild spirit passed over his limbs as though he were soaring sunward. His heart trembled in an ecstasy of fear and his soul was in flight. His soul was soaring in an air beyond the world and the body he knew was purified in a breath and delivered of incertitude and made radiant and commingled with the element of the spirit. An ecstasy of flight made radiant his eyes and wild his breath and tremulous and wild and radiant his windswept limbs.

So far, the passage has emphasized *self* to a very high degree. Now listen to what happens as the hero looks out upon the world in relation to himself, for he is "near to the wild heart of life":

> He started up nervously from the stoneblock for he could no longer quench the flame in his blood. He felt his cheeks aflame and his throat throbbing with song. There was a lust of wandering in his feet that burned to set out for the ends of the earth. On! On! his heart seemed to cry. Evening would deepen above the sea, night fall upon the plains, dawn glimmer before the wanderer and show him strange fields and hills and faces. Where?

In the course of his euphoric journey looking out upon the sea, he is suddenly transfixed by Eros:

A girl stood before him in midstream, alone and still, gazing out to sea. She seemed like one whom magic has changed into the likeness of a strange and beautiful seabird. Her long slender bare legs were delicate as a crane's and pure save where an emerald trail of seaweed had fashioned itself as a sign upon the flesh. Her thighs, fuller and softhued as ivory, were bared almost to the hips where the white fringes of her drawers were like feathering of soft white down. Her slateblue skirts were kilted boldly about her waist and dovetailed behind her. Her bosom was as a bird's, soft and slight, slight and soft as the breast of some darkplummaged dove. But her long fair hair was girlish: and girlish, and touched with the wonder of mortal beauty, her face.[11]

Enough for now. It is not far-fetched to see in visions like these an application of spirituality that should be within the reach of almost anyone.

UNITARIANS AND KINDRED MOVEMENTS CONSIDERED

There exists an institution that is particularly receptive to spiritual freedom: the Unitarian Universalist Church. Those who seek a free and independent form of spirituality may at some point or other consider the merits of belonging. It could be argued that this institution has, for all its merits, limitations.

Unitarianism traces its origins to the Apostolic Age of Christianity when theological disputes among bishops and presbyters led to the hammering out of Trinitarian doctrine as orthodoxy. The definitive events took place in the First Council of Nicaea, which met in AD 325. The Emperor Constantine intervened on the side of the Trinitarians. Unitarians trace their antecedents to the losers in that early theological showdown.

During the sixteenth century, the anti-Trinitarian views were revived by some early Protestant leaders, especially the Italian reformer Faustus Socinus (Fausto Sozzini), who eventually denied the divinity of Christ. After the Spanish theologian Michael Servetus was executed in Geneva on orders from John Calvin for questioning the doctrine of the Trinity, Socinus and others fled to Poland or other destinations in eastern Europe. "Unitarian" caught on as an English term for the doctrines of certain "Polish Brethren."

Unitarianism began to take hold and evolve. It gained a new momentum in the eighteenth-century Enlightenment. In the nineteenth century, the English and American Unitarian movement developed beyond its anti-Trinitarian roots and embraced a toleration that eventually challenged the orthodox insistence on the unique divine authority of scripture. It was only a matter of time before the Unitarian movement, though a nominally Christian form of worship, followed the example of Socinus and challenged the orthodox insistence on the divinity of Christ.

In 1961, the American Unitarian Association merged with the Universalist Church of America—a movement preaching universal salvation—thus creating the Unitarian Universalist Church. Unitarian Universalism has moved beyond its conceptual origins. It is a now a "non-creedal" community, a worldwide spiritual movement emphasizing intellectual freedom, toleration, egalitarian ideals, and the study of comparative religions as the basis for eclectic forms of worship. Even atheists are welcome.

The merits of Unitarian Universalism for spiritual "seekers" are obvious. And yet the movement has shortcomings.

For one thing, Unitarian doctrine has an optimistic slant that might strike the more tough-minded people as naïve. Unitarian hymns are suffused with the expectation of global harmony and millennial peace. Such visions run afoul of the persistent realities of human nature at its worst. For those who seek a spirituality that carries along with it a forthright engagement with evil, Unitarianism may seem like a dalliance with untenable and utopian expectations.

For another thing, the secular affinities of Unitarianism are sometimes frankly proclaimed to be "liberal." Many people within the Unitarian movement have labeled themselves as the bearers of "liberal religion." But *independent* worship should arguably be "non-creedal" in its secular affinities as well as its theology. It should therefore make more allowance for the thoughts, proclivities, preferences, and moods of maverick independents.

This critique of Unitarian culture might seem to be trifling compared with the benefits of the movement. Nonetheless, the still-evolving history of Unitarianism remains open-ended, and this situation suggests the possibility of a separate but derivative movement in the future.

Kindred movements have arisen to provide new channels for community and group participation among spiritual seekers.

In the 1870s, a movement arose to channel spiritual impulses into "non-theistic" belief. A key figure in the movement was Felix Adler, who founded the New York Society for Ethical Culture in 1876. Derivative organizations sprang up to promote "ethical" and "humanist" replacements for organized religion, among them the American Ethical Union and the American Humanist Association.

The Spiritual Naturalist Society traces its origins to the teachings of Joris-Karl Huysmans in the 1890s. It seeks to harmonize scientific "naturalism" with spirituality.

Among Quakers, a Humanist Society of Friends was created in the 1930s to apply the Quaker ethos in more adventurous ways. The tradition is promoted to this day by "Non-Theist Friends."

Depending on personal preferences, contemporary seekers may find one or more of these movements appealing.

ESOTERICA CONSIDERED

Within the overlapping religious traditions that are called "esoterica"—the word denotes practices and beliefs that are kept secret—there are groups of "alternative" doctrines that contribute in some ways to independent or speculative thinking in spiritual matters, if only to a limited extent.

One of these traditions—"Hermeticism"—has its roots in antiquity. But the others—Rosicrucianism, Theosophy, Spiritualism, and Anthroposophy—were created in the last half-millenium. "Hermeticism" got its name from "Hermes Trismegistus," a figure (perhaps mythical) to whom a body of lore was ascribed in the early centuries AD. A monotheistic tradition, Hermeticism was also a pastiche that blended contradictory elements of Gnosticism, reincarnation lore, astrology, alchemy, and other occult arts, mysteries, and pseudosciences.[12]

In the seventeenth century, an esoteric movement known as "Rosicrucianism" arose in Europe. Hermetic doctrines figured in its lore. The "rosy cross" symbolism helped to placate some Christian defenders of orthodoxy, but the movement strove to keep its distance amid the murderous religious wars that were ravaging Europe. The eclectic mixture of Rosicrucian beliefs would influence the movement of Freemasonry in later years.

In nineteenth-century America, a wide range of new spiritual belief systems arose, some of them flexible—Transcendentalism is a good example—and others prescriptive. Some were nothing more than cults, whereas others evolved into permanent new denominations of Christianity. This was the milieu that would generate Shakerism, Mormonism, Christian Science, and Spiritualism, the latter an occult art centered in communication with the dead via mediums and séances.

Another new religion dating to the mid-nineteenth century is the Baha'i Faith, a movement that preaches the essential unity of all religions. Lovely in its motivations, this faith has the very same weakness as Unitarianism: too much sweetness and light and insufficient tough-mindedness.

In 1875, a Russian immigrant named Helena Blavatsky founded the "Theosophical Society" in New York. Like other esoteric movements, Theosophy was deeply syncretistic. It was in many ways a hybrid of Hermeticism and elements of East Asian religions. Blavatsky claimed that an ancient "secret doctrine" was the underpinning of all the world's major religions and that this doctrine would gradually reemerge. Central to Theosophy was the belief in reincarnation, along with the belief that a messianic figure, manifested as both Christ and Krishna in the past, would continue to guide humanity toward enlightenment and brotherhood. Annie Besant, a successor of Blavatsky's, claimed in 1909 that an Indian boy named Jiddu Krishnamurti was the reborn messiah.

Importantly—for our purposes—Theosophy embraced the principle of dissent. Participants in the movement were free to engage in their own speculations. And so it was that in the early twentieth century a German Theosophist and esoteric teacher named Rudolf Steiner broke away from Theosophy and founded a new esoteric movement that he called "Anthroposophy."

A gifted architect and a major contributor to the field of progressive education, Steiner embraced intellectual and spiritual freedom. Like other esotericists, he tried to bridge the worlds of spirituality and science, claiming that through meditative practice one can achieve the sort of knowledge that, like mathematics, does not depend on sensory perceptions. And like many other esotericists, he embraced unprovable doctrines such as reincarnation and clairvoyance. He indulged in the kind of speculation that utilizes myths.

The liberating side of Theosophy and Anthroposophy—both of which are still in existence—is their emphasis on speculative freedom and their toleration of dissent. Their tolerant side stands in contrast to the openly authoritarian character of cults such as Scientology. But like other esoteric traditions, Theosophy and Anthroposophy are grounded in elements of false certitude. Belief in reincarnation provides a demonstration. The doctrine is in some ways a very pleasant fantasy, but it can never be proven, no matter how ardently its adherents want to believe in it. It is also fraught with severe conceptual problems, not least of all by the standards of biological science.

Nonetheless, for all of their weaknesses, the esoteric movements have sometimes lent themselves to responsible forms of speculation.

In the early twentieth century, a Russo-Greek-Armenian esotericist named George Ivanovich Gurdjieff gathered a substantial group of followers around teachings that were drawn from the Hermetic tradition. Each follower was encouraged to pursue his or her own individual speculations, and the movement as a whole was known as "the Work."

Some of the participants had valid scientific credentials and their speculations were cogent. Their theories can never be proven, but some of them intersect mysteries that every thinking person may confront, especially the time enigma. Reincarnation in Hermeticism leads often to the notions of "eternal recurrence" or "circular time" that can interpenetrate multidimensional time. Indeed, a Russian member of the movement, Peter Ouspensky, came up with a conception of multidimensional time in which *all* of the dimensions are circular.

The previously mentioned British mathematician John G. Bennett, with his theory of three-dimensional time, was influenced by the Work, and a Jungian psychiatrist named Maurice Nicoll was a full-fledged participant. In his book *Living Time*, Nicoll presented an unorthodox time proposition, which, while not wholly original, was nonetheless striking. He advanced the idea of an "eternal Now" that is different from the thing that we know as "the present moment," though it also includes it.

"*Now*," he wrote, "contains all time, all the life, and the aeon of life. [...] We must understand that what we call the present moment is not *now*, for the present moment is on the horizontal line of time and now is vertical to this and incommensurable with it."[13] This visualization of multidimensional time is *rectilinear* rather than circular. John Bennett the mathematician embraced this particular visualization with his theory of a full-fledged "eternity axis" that is "perpendicular" to other time dimensions.[14] The Swedish-American astronomer Gustaf Strömberg envisioned an "eternity domain" that is outside of the fabric of space-time but also connected with it.[15]

Out of this milieu came something of a literary movement using time as its mystical theme. Plays like John Balderston's *Berkeley Square* (1928) and J. B. Priestley's so-called time plays of the 1930s—plays built around the mystic implications of the "déjà vu" experience—brought esoteric themes to mass culture. So did films making use of the "time problem" in plots that were starkly metaphysical. Among the seminal examples of this cinematic genre were *Portrait of Jennie* (1948) and *Somewhere in Time* (1980). Both of these films became "cult classics," and both of them used the theme of time travel as the basis for tales of tragic love. Such Hollywood productions coaxed millions of viewers into moods that were intensely spiritual—moods that commanded more excitement and emotional power (perhaps) than the regular rituals of worship.

Tales of lovers from different time dimensions brought moviegoers face to face with the ghostliness of life. And the overlapping influence of science fiction in this form of spirituality should not be overlooked.

These popular productions were a form of "underground religion." Moviegoers were thinking for themselves—thinking for themselves far more than they could manage during regular attendance in church.[16]

ECKHART TOLLE AND *THE POWER OF NOW*

Spiritual teachers, as they call themselves, come and go, and many turn out to be deranged—or tyrannical. But one of the most interesting and wholesome in recent years is the German-born Canadian writer Eckhart Tolle. His 1999 book *The Power of Now* became a best seller with a simple and potent message: we need to live and experience spirituality in the present moment.

But there was more. Drawing on a number of themes from the Buddhist tradition, Tolle preached the idea of renunciation as a pathway to peace. He engaged in metaphysical speculation—though he never acknowledged it as speculation.

He recommended an inward surrender to the all-encompassing and transcendent power of *Now*. He preached cessation of mental activity—especially critical analysis—and the casting aside of our time sense.

"Free yourself from your mind," Tolle wrote, because the effort to accomplish this is the "only true liberation."[17] To grasp the ineffability of *being*, we must stifle our impulse to *think* about it, and instead just *commune* with it through a nonrational experience. "Being is the ever-present One Life beyond the myriad forms of life," he explained, but "don't seek to grasp it with your mind" and "don't try to understand it."[18]

To achieve this mental transformation—to *transcend* the mental process—we must cast away our inner sense of time. You may think that "the past gives you an identity and the future holds the promise of salvation," Tolle wrote, but both past and future "are illusions." Time "isn't precious at all, because it is an illusion. What you perceive as precious is not time but the one point that is out of time: the Now." After all, he reasons, "nothing ever happened in the past; it happened in the Now." By the same token, "nothing will ever happen in the future; it will happen in the Now."[19]

Liberation from pain and suffering will come if we can glory in—and surrender to—*now* every moment, for the power that *now* represents cannot be canceled, no matter what happens: "Fear cannot prevail against it."[20]

Tolle hastened to explain that he is not recommending a life of passivity. "Any action is better than no action," he affirmed, so if there is something that you ought to be doing, "get up and do it now." But if action does not yield significant results, then surrender is the wisest thing to do. If disaster strikes, "know that there is another side to it" and that surrender is never defeat. "I do not mean to say that you will become happy in such a situation," he admitted, for "you will not," but your "fear and pain will become transmuted into an inner peace."[21]

To which one is tempted to reply with one single word: maybe.

There is something to be said for the system that Tolle recommends. The power to find peace in catastrophe will depend upon the fortitude—and the psychological make-up—of different people. In hopeless situations, his method may well be justifiable.

And it is excellent to say, as Tolle does, that the truth about *being* will continue to elude us no matter how hard we try to understand it.

Notwithstanding its virtues, however, Tolle's system has problems.

The notion that we can ever completely transcend the activity of mind is inadmissible: try as we might to achieve such a state—a state "beyond mind"— our identity *does* inhere in mind, and there is no way around the situation. Moreover, the renunciation of critical analysis is never wise.

While Tolle disavows the intention to advocate a life of passivity, too great an adherence to his teachings might blind us to possibilities for action that could shape the future—shape it by altering the paths of contingency in ways that could make the world better. It is right to stress, as Tolle does, that "the future" as it constantly arrives will be *rendered* in the medium of *now*. But to dismiss "the future" as "illusion" can lead to tragedy.

INDEPENDENCE: A BEGINNING AND A METHOD

Regardless, Tolle's emphasis upon the ontological primacy of *now* is an excellent beginning for those who seek spirituality. Let us therefore build upon it. What follows is a method for attaining a spiritual mood that almost anyone can use independently.

Begin like this: put yourself in a meditative state and then concentrate upon *your awareness*. *Feel* this awareness in the ever-present *now*, which is the fact that is *presenting your existence*. You are *bound* to it. It connects you to everything else. Dwell upon the fact.

Dwell upon it *analytically* as you dwell upon it *intuitively*, for these activities must overlap.

Now is the *bond* that connects you to *the force behind everything*—and so explore it. *This fact* is a link between yourself and the force behind existence that we constantly *feel*. It *proves* existence.

It is proof that both you and the cosmos are *real*, and that reality *transcends any logic*. Unbelievable? Some people might find it that way, by the terms of their own brand of logic—yet *it is*.

Because the power of *now* is *self-evident*.

So what if everything that happens has to happen—unlikely as it seems?

Would our wonder at existing be less?

The message of Schopenhauer will in any event be proven wrong, since the cosmos is *something*. Let us definitely call the world *that*. We are part of a force that in his view "shouldn't be here."

Yet it *is*.

Reality is like a *magic spell*.

CHAPTER 6

THE MISUSE OF SPIRITUALITY

Reality is … "like a magic spell?"

Anyone advancing a claim like that is on extremely dangerous ground. But religion can be dangerous. Rationality—like civilization—is fragile, and humanity has struggled for years to protect itself from the delusions and the outright insanity that people can succumb to. The scientific method is a fundamental form of self-defense.

But even scientists confront the uncanny when they try to account for the metaphysics that "quantum" phenomena imply. And when they go on to acknowledge the mystery of "being," they conclude (for very good reason) that mysteries like that are *beyond the reach* of science.

The exercise of coming to terms with the experience of *now* may be offered as an ontic *moment of truth* that can help as we try to reconcile mysticism and reason. To say that reality is *like* a magic spell does not mean that it *is* a magic spell and it does not justify hallucinatory forms of religion.

But it can lead to them.

The misuse of religion and spirituality is an age-old story of tyranny, psychopathology, and scandal. The history of spirituality is to a great extent the history of persecution. Mystical moments are absorbed into underlying mental conditions of derangement that generate cruelty, fanaticism, and obsession.

The only thing that holds out the possibility for redemption in spiritual matters is *freedom*—not only the freedom to think independently and fairly but the freedom of others to do the same.

A SOPHISTICATE'S ASSESSMENT OF "GOD"

About a quarter century ago, a former nun and lapsed Roman Catholic named Karen Armstrong wrote a learned and very popular history of Judaism, Christianity, and Islam. *A History of God* was her title, and she opened the book with a candid confession: the description of God that was force-fed to her in childhood was a stultifying force from which she struggled to free herself for years.

"God is the Supreme Spirit, Who alone exists of Himself and is infinite in all perfections." That was the definition she had to memorize in church and in the cloister, and it always, she declared, "seemed a singularly arid, pompous and arrogant definition." It still, she added, "leaves me cold," and she came to the conclusion that it is also intrinsically "incorrect."[1]

But what is "correct?"

She surveyed the vast range of different spiritual systems that have come and gone as people try to come to terms with "the divine," and she concluded that for all the orthodoxies that arise, there will always remain a residual "pragmatism" in the human spirit that will seek to assert itself eventually. "It is far more important," she wrote, "for a particular idea of God to *work* than for it to be logically or scientifically sound. As soon as it ceases to be effective it will be changed—sometimes for something radically different."[2]

Turning to the question of what "works best" for modern spiritual seekers, she deplored the fundamentalism that can make religious life so primitive. If we project too much of our own expectations into concepts of God, she argued, we create extremely childish visions of a "personalized" deity that cannot do justice to the magnitude of mystery that we are confronting. Instead, we should "learn that God does not exist in any simplistic sense" and that "the very word 'God' is only a symbol of a reality that ineffably transcends it."[3]

What we struggle to understand as "God," she suggested, is essentially "a reality of an entirely different order."[4]

She reviewed the work of philosophers, theologians, and scientists who have guided the world of opinion as they ponder that "different order." And one of the most influential was Martin Heidegger—he who studied the problems and the paradoxes of "being."

The work of Heidegger was indeed fundamentally important. But it was also fraught with painful lessons.

TWO VERY DIFFERENT GERMANS

It is incontestable that Heidegger made an invaluable contribution to spirituality by returning to the "fundamental ontology" of Parmenides and exploring it for the benefit of modern sensibilities.

Yet he may have achieved something else: he might have shown for all time how the spiritual impulse can go very wrong in certain people who are otherwise very gifted thinkers. For Heidegger joined the Nazi Party.

Admirers of Heidegger within the field of philosophy often brush aside his Nazism as inconsequential. They presume that he said some things that he never believed so he could stay in his native country and continue to teach.

But upon his election as rector of Freiburg University in 1933, he delivered an inaugural lecture that was fraught with allegiance to Nazi principles and steeped in the cultural presuppositions of its feral ideology: the bogus metaphysics of "blood and soil," the uses of primitivism in establishing certitude, and the necessity of indoctrination. The intellectual scandal of Heidegger is a subject that has generated copious analysis.[5]

The contrast between his Nazi pronouncements and the delicacy of his *Being and Time* is shocking. But it reminds us that the human mind can succumb to all sorts of weird contradictions since the *moods* that suffuse human thinking are sometimes perverse beyond belief. And these moods can pervade an entire intellectual milieu. A strain of anti-rational primitivism was an unmistakable presence in certain subcurrents of German philosophic thinking from Fichte to Nietzsche.

Anti-rationality is on the cusp of "mysticism," and the problem is germane to the dangers of spirituality. "Rational spirituality" might seem to be a kind of oxymoron, but the difference between the value-neutral word "mysticism" and the highly pejorative word "irrationality" is telling. Any form of thinking— whether putatively rational or not—can be abused, and we must therefore draw upon all the resources of conscience, analytical scrutiny, fair-mindedness, and candor to hold our own against the danger.

Arguably, the mystical potentiality in Heidegger's thinking went terribly wrong.

His book *An Introduction to Metaphysics* began as a series of lectures that he gave in the summer of 1935. He criticized the "halves and inadequacies" that were in his opinion ruining modern thought, and declared that "in essential matters halves are more disastrous than the so-called nothingness." Ambiguities must therefore yield to *totalities*, and in that very spirit Nazism should purify itself more and more. "The works that are being peddled about nowadays as the philosophy of National Socialism," he wrote, were inadequate, for as yet they had "nothing whatever to do with the inner truth and greatness of this movement (namely the encounter between global technology and modern man)."[6]

Heidegger's defenders are quick to conclude that this testimonial to the "inner truth and greatness" of Nazism was nothing more than an obligatory gesture to keep the Gestapo at bay. Perhaps it was.

Or perhaps it was evidence that Heidegger, in his quest to transcend "forgetfulness of being," was seduced by the hypnotic power of Nazi oratory, by the "Volksgemeinschaft" (communal belonging) of its pageantry, by the delirium that charisma sometimes engenders. Is that what occurred? Could it be that in the throes of these conditions he came to the intuitive conclusion that only a *forceful* certitude such as Hitler's—brutally forceful—could put one *forcefully* in touch with the primal nature of "being?" Is that truly what happened?

We may never know.

But the possibility should serve as a reminder that even sophisticated spirituality can lapse into perversion and become simple-minded and vicious.

In contrast to Martin Heidegger's choices, an equally lofty German intellectual came to opposite conclusions about spirituality in the course of the 1930s—not an anti-Nazi cleric like Dietrich Bonhoeffer but a literary figure who claimed that metaphysical imperatives exalt the cause of freedom. He came close to arguing that freedom is the strongest and the most basic of spiritual forces.

The novelist Thomas Mann went into exile and came to America after fleeing from Germany. In 1938, he traveled throughout the United States giving lectures in English—later published in book form under the title *The Coming Victory of Democracy*. He exhorted Americans to wake from their slumber and rediscover the incipient *power* of democratic values. The force of his arguments derived from spirituality.

Whereas Heidegger criticized "forgetfulness of being," Mann criticized the forgetfulness of *human dignity*. He also criticized an existential form of forgetfulness among defenders of freedom. Democracy, he said, "should put aside the habit of taking itself for granted, of self-forgetfulness. It should use this wholly unexpected situation—the fact, namely, that it has again become problematical—to renew and rejuvenate itself by again becoming aware of itself."[7]

Democracy is grounded in "the dignity of mankind" *for spiritual reasons.* "It is," he declared, "for its own spiritualization that nature produced mankind."[8] Democracy "wishes to elevate mankind, to teach it to think, to set it free."[9] Fascism is grounded in nothing more than a base "lust for degradation which it would be too much honor to call devilish, for it is simply diseased."[10] And democracy can cure this disease because "democracy's resources of vitality and youthfulness cannot be overestimated," whereas "the youthful insolence of fascism is a mere grimace." Democracy is "timelessly human," whereas tyranny is inherently "transitory."[11]

ATROCITIES

Cruelty and religion have existed in savage and unholy combinations since time immemorial. The misuse of spirituality as a pretext for indulging the worst pathologies of the mind—sadism, blood lust, necrophilia—is a consequence of our evolved human nature at its worst. Sick fanatics can easily turn rituals of "purification" into blatant opportunities for slaughter—and desecration.

Of course, if people weren't killing each other for religious reasons, they would find other reasons. The human experience is ruined all the time by malevolent predation, and religious war is just another variation of the boundless human propensity for making life miserable. The same can be said of religious persecution: if people weren't hating each other in the name of God, they would find other reasons for hate.

But the historical record of religious war and religious persecution is stunning. The Middle East in recent years was the global epicenter, and the hatred spread outward in attacks upon innocent people by ISIS (Islamic State of Iraq and Syria) fanatics in many other parts of the world. But a generation ago, Northern Ireland was bloodied by the enmity of Catholics and Protestants, which goes all the way back to the religious wars of the sixteenth century. Christian aggression toward Judaism and Islam is a very old story, and the Christian "re-conquest" of Islamic Spain—in many ways a haven of toleration and enlightenment—was a tragic process. Anti-Semitism is a scourge that has blackened Christianity for many years.

Put bluntly, religion often serves as a "cover"—or excuse—for a hellish brutality in human nature, for pathological urges that can best be described as a sickness (though of course there are other ways to describe them).

In his book *The Anatomy of Human Destructiveness*, the psychiatrist Erich Fromm asserted that "what is unique in man is that he can be driven by impulses to kill and to torture, *and that he feels lust in doing so* [emphasis added]."[12]

The assertion was arguable, since we can never gain *direct access* to the innermost feelings of others—we can never directly *partake* of the mental life of others, especially other species. The feeling of "lust" in the infliction of torture may be common in the life of other animals. But its reality in human affairs is made obvious every single day.

Fromm's discourse on the forms of "ecstatic destructiveness" that patients have revealed to their psychiatrists, including the *ecstasies* of sadism—the "trance-like state" that can result from acts that hurt, degrade, control, and humiliate others—must be worthy of credence. When patients *describe* such feelings in therapeutic sessions, there can be little doubt that they are very sick people indeed.

Beyond sadism—and masochism, which of course is the obverse of sadism—Fromm analyzed "necrophilious" forms of perversion, which appear to derive from a weird "attraction to what is dead and putrid." This attraction can sometimes escalate into a "pure passion to destroy"—the passion to *make* things dead, nonexistent, or putrid.[13]

It is possible to wonder whether lusts like these, when they occur in the minds of fanatics, may amount to a secret form of "death worship"—*secret* because such believers pretend that their acts are uplifting exercises, when in fact they are something very different.

We can only guess what feelings were flowing through the minds of the Aztecs when they committed human sacrifice—to "appease the gods." We can only surmise what delight was being sought (and achieved) by the ISIS terrorists as they went about beheading people in Iraq. Or by the al-Qaeda murderers as they flew the airliners full of screaming and helpless people into the skyscrapers.

Who can say what passions were felt by the Catholic Inquisitors as they mutilated "heretics" and burned them at the stake—or by the Kamikaze pilots who obliterated themselves and shiploads of sailors in devotion to a latter-day perversion of the Japanese Shinto religion? There are many different lethal or obscene misuses of religion, but most of them derive from the force of psychopathologies seeking an outlet.

Perhaps it is neither here nor there, but the monotheistic religions seem to have a penchant for bloody persecution. The ancient Romans, martial though they were, were receptive to the deities of other polytheistic religions. The goddess Isis, for instance, was welcomed into the Roman pantheon and a potent Isis cult sprang up in imperial Rome. The principle was straightforward: when the Romans encountered other polytheistic systems, they embraced the new deities because they represented new augmentations of power—supernatural power—that could be brought into the service of Rome.

Compare this attitude to the jealous vehemence of the ancient Hebrews' God Yahweh, who would brook no competition at all when it came to the prerogatives of loyalty and worship. Elijah, after summoning Yahweh to perform a series of edifying power demonstrations for the Israelites, told his followers to capture all the priests of the Canaanite god Baal and put them to death.

The dictatorial potentialities of a creed that is built around a single deity who holds universal sway have been demonstrated over and over again in the bloody and tyrannical deeds of monotheistic worshippers: if there is ONE TRUE GOD, such believers tend to say, there is ONE TRUE WAY—the way of the Lord—that must be forced upon everyone on earth.

And woe to any skeptics who resist.

Hence the nasty, dictatorial words that are put into the mouth of Jesus in the Gospel of John (8:42–44):

> Jesus said unto them, If God were your Father, ye would love me: for I proceeded forth and came from God. [...] Ye are of your father the devil, and the lusts of your father ye will do. He was a murderer from the beginning, and abode not in the truth, because there is no truth in him. [...] And because I tell you the truth, ye believe me not [...] because ye are not of God.

Not of God ... children of the devil ... those who refuse to submit must be chastised—and damned to torment—in the name of all that is holy. In this manner, the teachings of Jesus as rendered in the Gospel of John (surely a "saint" in name only, whoever he was) take us straight down the years to the Salem witchcraft trials of 1692, to say nothing of the Anti-Semitic pogroms that have been perpetrated for centuries in the name of Christ by murderous thugs.[14]

Enthusiasts for monotheistic religion often tout it as a unifying force for decent values—a force that emphasizes "what we all have in common" and therefore promotes human dignity. Such enthusiasts find it all the more shocking when they suddenly observe how the ways of monotheistic religion can degenerate into horror.

The perpetrators of the horror are perforce in their own minds innocent and pure: victims of the ugly unbelievers. Hence the darkly hilarious spectacle of American evangelical Christians who steadily complain that their "right" to "practice their faith" is denied by whoever resists them as they dish out orders to everyone else—resists them as they try to tell everybody else in the land what to do and believe.

The same could be said of the Islamic fanatics who believe that the *very existence* of democratic values anywhere in the world is an attack upon the sanctity of their own faith that demands violent vengeance.

The barbarity and tyranny of organized religion at its worst should not blind us to its good points. But would it not be better for the world if its spiritual communities relinquished mythology, confessed that the truth about the source of *being* is ineffable, and sought fulfillment in more enlightened ways?

CHAPTER 7

PARADIGMS OF GOD

Karen Armstrong wrote in the 1990s that "the idols of fundamentalism are not good substitutes for God," and that "if we are to create a vibrant new faith for the twenty-first century, we should [...] ponder the history of God for some lessons and warnings." One of the lessons is that "God does not exist in any simplistic sense" and that "the very word 'God' is only a symbol of a reality that ineffably transcends it." Consequently, we should "acquire a restraint that stops us rushing into these matters with dogmatic assurance."[1]

In light of that perspective, her history of the monotheistic traditions of Judaism, Christianity, and Islam was fraught with something of a paradox.

On the one hand, her history showed that some of the theologians who have exerted the greatest influence on these faiths were in near-unanimous agreement with her view that our minds are incapable of grasping the truth about divinity. So far from being a modern or nontraditional insight, the view that God's nature is completely unfathomable to the human mind has been embraced by one theologian after another down the centuries.

Indeed, this view has been so common among the monotheistic theologians that it is almost a cliché.

On the other hand, these same theologians went on to *attempt* what they said was impossible: they attempted to build a convincing "diagram" of God's nature, and many of them did it with insufferable self-assurance.

Such hypocrisy can be a rich and amusing subject for satire if we choose to view it that way. But the spectacle of countless theologians "rushing in where angels fear to tread" reveals a fact about the human mind that is in certain ways more poignant than outrageous: our *curiosity* about the mystery that underlies existence is so powerful that we are prompted to push our conceptual powers to the limit. And there is nothing necessarily wrong with an effort to probe the possibilities regarding "God's nature" so long as the exercise is frankly and admittedly speculative.

That was one of the very best things about the theory of a "dipolar God" that was offered by Alfred North Whitehead: to his everlasting credit, he admitted that his exercise was totally *speculative*.

Such humility, alas, has not often been reflected in the work of the monotheistic theologians. To the contrary: they have built the constructions of their minds into dogmas with such tyrannical authority that those who refused to submit were sometimes put to death.

The Christian doctrine of the Trinity provides a good example.

The doctrine of three "persons" within the "Godhead" has seemed rather ludicrous to Muslims, Jews, and many others. And when taken on the level of mythology and superstition, the doctrine *is* ludicrous. But if the labels "God the Father, God the Son, and God the Holy Ghost" are taken as metaphors or representational *aspects* of divinity—as the minds of some people conceptualize it—then the doctrine of the Trinity becomes more comprehensible when analyzed from the standpoint of ontology.

If we put our conceptual powers to work, we may infer that the *source* of existence, the *source* of the cosmos, the *source* of ourselves, is something *other* than the manifest contents of the cosmos. This might be called the concept of *transcendence* as applied to the force behind existence, the "otherness" of whatever it is that accounts for the world. So principle number one as applied to the "Godhead" is *transcendence*.

But then, if we consider that the cosmos is *active*, we may come to the conclusion that however transcendent the force behind existence may be, it is also *creative*, and this creativity must work as a kind of *emanation*. So principle number two is *emanation*. And if we think to ourselves that the force behind existence must be *present* somehow within the cosmic process—*implicit* in the very fact of existence—we have hit upon the doctrine of *immanence*, which is principle number three.

These ideas *prove absolutely nothing* in regard to the mystery of *being*. But they are predictable. In some ways they are almost *inevitable* creations of the human mind—normal, as it were—since the structure of our minds and the ontic experience of life that we are given make us generate these kinds of ideas *at least some of the time*.

We might as well admit that these ideas are quite *interesting*, though they may—for all we know—be quite false. Regardless, in terms of intellectual history, they *account* for the doctrine of the Trinity, as early Christian theologians developed it, with "God the Father" representing *transcendence*, "God the Son" representing creative *emanation or emergence*, and "God the Holy Ghost" representing *immanence*.

All of these constructions of the human mind are quite normal and interesting—perhaps enlightening. But as *dogma*, they are totally *absurd* since they *prove nothing*.

EMANATION

The concept of divine "emanation" or "emergence" is perhaps the most predictable notion in regard to the "workings" of God. An early example may be found in a Greco-Jewish speculation that was produced in the first century BC, the so-called Wisdom Literature. The most famous version was a tract called *The Wisdom of Solomon.* "Wisdom" was presented as an emanation that manifests God's activity in the world. "Wisdom" was also *personified*—personified in female form and given the Greek name "Sophia." This surely suggests the Greek myth in which Athena, the goddess of wisdom, emanates from the forehead of Zeus, her father, and the adaptation of this theme in a production associated with "Solomon" is a very good example of Hellenistic-Hebraic syncretism.

This syncretism would continue, and it shaped the development of early Christianity. The emanative principle of "Wisdom" or "Sophia" was transmuted into "Logos"—the "Word"—by the Jewish philosopher Philo of Alexandria, who died ca. AD 50, and the concept was borrowed by the author of the Gospel of John, who wrote that God the Son is indeed Logos, and that Jesus was the incarnate embodiment of Logos. The doctrine was taken up by such early Christian theologians as Clement, Irenaeus, and Origen, and it was orthodoxy by the time that the trinitarian doctrine was hammered into place in the Council of Nicaea.

The Roman philosopher Plotinus, who wrote in the third century AD, was one of the most influential thinkers in the West who developed the theology of emanation. He taught that from a primal unity came two successive emanations, the first of them masculine and the second feminine, both denoted by Greek names. The first emanation, Mind, was called *nous*, and the second, Soul, was called *psyche*. Plotinus had this to say about the reason for divine emanation:

> The One is perfect because it seeks for nothing, and possesses nothing, and has need of nothing; and being perfect, it overflows, and thus its superabundance produces an Other. [...] Whenever anything reaches its own perfection, we see that it cannot endure to remain in itself, but generates and produces some other thing. [...] How then should the Most Perfect Being and the First Good remain shut up in itself, as though it were jealous or impotent?[2]

How indeed? This presupposition can be traced to the *Timaeus* of Plato, written centuries earlier, and Plotinus, like many other so-called Neoplatonists, embraced it. The idea of an Absolute that is driven by its nature to generate and interact with an "Other" would be integral to many metaphysical systems in later years, not least of all Hegelianism.

In the early sixth century, four mystical treatises of immense influence were produced by a Christian writer who took the name "Dionysius the Areopagite." The "Dionysius" in question was a Greek who was converted to Christianity (according to *Acts of the Apostles*) by St. Paul in a sermon that he preached on the hill of Areopagus outside Athens. But the sixth-century writer is now universally identified as "Pseudo-Dionysius" (or "Pseudo-Denys") because in time it was obvious that the tracts were written centuries after the death of the original "Areopagite."

Pseudo-Dionysius argued that God is essentially "dipolar," with the "far side" turned away from the world and locked forever in self-contemplation. This hidden side of God is a realm of unfathomable mystery, so inscrutable in its nature that we would be just as well advised to call it "Nothing" as opposed to any "Something" that we might be able to understand as "existence" in everyday usage.

It bears noting that the method of explaining God in terms of negatives ("Via Negativa"), even when taken to the rhetorical extreme of calling him "Nothing," is in some ways comparable to the doctrine of "Sunyata"—or the "Void"—in the theology of Mahayana Buddhism. We shall have more to observe in due course about "nothingness" and "void," but the relationship between these early doctrines and the latter-day philosophy of Schopenhauer is obvious.

But Pseudo-Dionysius also embraced the emanation doctrine when he wrote that the side of God that is *turned toward the world* overflows in a joyous "ecstasis" that is going on continuously.

One theologian after another in the centuries that followed would embrace this duality. They would avow that God "as he is in himself" is inscrutable, but that he "overflows" in a manner that creates the world we know. The Islamic scholar Abu Nasr al-Farabi, who died ca. AD 980, wrote that God's emanations can be traced with great precision though no fewer than ten distinct heavenly spheres. This doctrine was reiterated and amplified by the famous Abu Ali Ibn-Sina or "Avicenna" (980–1037), who argued that the emanations consist of pure "imagination," which is then concretized as it descends until it reaches our world via Gabriel, the spirit of Revelation.

Down through the eighteenth century and beyond, this doctrine remained influential. Perhaps the most memorable version of it was presented in verse by Alexander Pope:

Vast chain of being, which from God began,

Natures aethereal, human, angel, man,

Beast, bird, fish, insect! what no eye can see,

No glass can reach! From Infinite to thee.[3]

Perhaps the most elaborate formulation of the emanation doctrine can be found in the Jewish Kabbalah, a body of metaphorical and mystical lore that took shape in the Middle Ages, though it drew upon much earlier speculation. It forms one of the most explicit precedents for modern "process theology," since it envisions the progressive evolution of God. One of the surviving sources of Kabbalistic doctrine is the *Zohar*, written by the Spanish Jew Moses of Leon in the thirteenth century. The sixteenth-century Kabbalistic doctrines of Isaac Luria were written down by a disciple named Kayim Vital under the title *Etz Hayim* (The Tree of Life).

In the Kabbalistic system, the essence of God-the-unknowable is called "En Sof." But En Sof progressively "made himself known" through a series of 10 emanations called "sefiroth," which could be understood as supernatural "names" for his own inner attributes, as for instance "Kether Elyon" (the Supreme Crown), "Hokhmah" (wisdom), "Binah" (intelligence), "Hesed" (love), "Din" (the power of severe judgment), and so on. The sefiroth spread downward from the Godhead in a pattern that is sometimes visualized in the form of an inverted tree, and they interpenetrate everything. In other versions of the Kabbalah, the emanations are visualized in the form of a vast human body.

In the *Zohar*, the descending sefiroth take on successive gender identities whose sex-like interaction spawns the world, and they emanate from the body and limbs of a primordial man, "Adam Kadmon," through whom the world is created.

Evil is explained in the doctrines of Luria as a combination of divine evolution and accident. En Sof, the unfathomable Godhead, purified itself somehow by creating a region of "nothingness" or "un-self" to which "Din," the stern power of judgment or wrath, was consigned. Separated from the rest of the Godhead, Din becomes destructive, especially since the process of emanation draws it out from the realm of "un-self" and projects it, along with all the other sefiroth, through Adam Kadmon.

Through some sort of a catastrophe, the lower six sefiroth (including Din) broke and then scattered chaotically when projected from the "eyes" of Adam Kadmon. The scattered fragments of projected "light" become trapped in a world of outer chaos. This teaching of Luria aligns closely with Gnosticism, and the damage to the first emanations from En Sof will be accordingly corrected through "Tikkun," or reintegration, a redemptive process through which En Sof will effectuate healing and repair.[4] Kabbalistic teaching would gradually embrace the idea that human action can *help* God effectuate repair through the rescue of scattered points of light.

Some biblical scholars believe that these Kabbalistic notions were prefigured in earlier Jewish occultism and that the Christology of St. Paul should be understood in this light. In this particular view, St. Paul may have come to the conclusion that God the Son (later to be identified as "Logos" by St. John) was in fact Adam Kadmon and that the incarnation and resurrection of Christ were pivotal events in the process of Tikkun or repair. One scholar, Hugh Schonfield, once speculated that when Christ is visually "transfigured" before his disciples, he is revealed in the vast and radiant dimensions of Adam Kadmon, the primordial man.[5]

In any case, by the nineteenth century, the idea that God's nature is evolving was embodied in the philosophy of Friedrich Wilhelm Joseph von Schelling, who put the matter this way in 1809:

> Has creation a final goal? And if so, why was it not reached at once? Why was the consummation not reached from the beginning? To these questions there is but one answer: Because God is *Life*, and not merely being. All life has a *fate*, and is subject to suffering and to becoming. To this, then, God has of his own free will subjected himself. [...] Being is *sensible* only in becoming. In being, as such, it is true, there is no becoming; in the latter, rather, it is itself posited as eternity. But in the actualization of being through opposition there is necessarily a becoming. Without the conception of a humanly suffering God [...] history remains wholly unintelligible.[6]

A century later, Henri Bergson in *L'Évolution créatrice* put forth the doctrine that God is the source of an evolving "life force." He described God as "a center from which worlds shoot out like rockets in a fireworks display," adding that God in his view "has nothing of the already made; he is unceasing life, action, freedom."[7] At this point the concept of divine emanation shades over into a vision of outright pantheism—or something very close to it.[8]

In any event, the long history of "emanation" as a concept in divinity shows that the movement for "process theology" in the twentieth century was building on many centuries' worth of antecedents.

BEING AND NOTHING

The speculations of the various theologians that were just presented were combinations of rationalism and myth. As religious *folklore*, they are *interesting*—every single one of them—but as practical guides they are mostly useless.

And as dogma, they are totally insufferable, for they *prove nothing*.

There is certainly a place for metaphor and poetry in responsible religious thinking, especially for mystics. More on that later. No insistence on rhetorical and analytical intelligibility can lessen the power of religious poetry—or lessen its power to *move us*. Beyond the many famous passages in Scripture, this brief composition by William Blake is both clever and surpassingly pretty:

> The Atoms of Democritus
> And Newton's Particles of light
> Are sands upon the Red Sea shore,
> Where Israel's tents do shine so bright.[9]

But unless we are willing to *surrender ourselves* to the artistic passions of others, we have to insist that their religious conceptions should meet a fundamental standard: they have to *make sense* under critical scrutiny. Such insistence is the sine qua non of independent spirituality.

The concept of divine emanation *does* withstand preliminary scrutiny—it *is* intelligible in ontological terms—because it flows from an issue that has always prompted thinking people to reflect upon religious themes: our sense that there is something *beyond* our experience, an *otherness* that is somehow more fundamental and *real* than the cosmos we inhabit—something that *accounts* for the existence of the cosmos.

Atheists presume that there is no such thing, but the rest of us continue to speculate and wonder.

Once again, we must emphasize the theme: our minds are very limited in their power to conceptualize *anything*, let alone metaphysical concepts. Even when it comes to the issues of science, we can only apprehend a very limited range of the natural frequencies (sound waves, for instance) that we *know* to be present. Our senses are powerful enough for our everyday uses. But their range is severely limited due to the nature of human biology—to the vagaries of human evolution.

The issues of abstract thinking make the problem even more severe. The search is now on to find hidden dimensions that our senses can never perceive and that our minds can only dimly apprehend with the aid of mathematics.

Remembering that, we should carefully ponder two ontological terms that are common in speculations about divinity: "Being" and "Nothing." To align with the usage of others—especially the commentators whose views will be cited momentarily—these terms will now be capitalized.

"Being"—a term that has figured so heavily in this account thus far—may be understood in different senses. And there is one sense in which monotheistic theologians have used the term that is fraught with difficulties: the tendency of some to apply the term in a *static* sense to a "Being" who is held to be eternal, unchanging, absolute, and immaculately perfect. Both St. Augustine and St. Thomas Aquinas used the term in this fundamental sense. The latter philosopher applied it from the teachings of Aristotle, which were lost to the West in the so-called Dark Ages, but recovered by scholars in Islamic Spain and made available to Christian theologians. Aquinas was eager to apply the Aristotelian concepts to Christianity.

Aristotle's "Prime Mover"—the static "Unmoved Mover" of his *Metaphysics*—was an archetype for the notion of "Being" that would influence Thomas Aquinas. But earlier philosophers viewed "Being" as a more comprehensive and pervasive "thing" than a magnetic "Unmoved Mover"—Parmenides, for instance, insofar as we can reconstruct his views from surviving written fragments.

In the eleventh century, Anselm of Canterbury constructed an "ontological proof" of the existence of God, and it went like this: God is something so great that *nothing greater can be thought*. And since existence is arguably "better" than nonexistence, God must be "Perfect Being"—whatever that is.

Anselm was reacting against the tradition that called God "Nothing," a tradition in the West that has a number of counterparts in the East. Shock value aside, this "Via Negativa" must to some extent be regarded as a form of poetic license, a *geste scandaleux à provoquer* that can guide the contemplative believer through problems that defy quick articulation.

The issue is God's ineffability. He is an entity beyond the power of the human mind to grasp, if he can truly be said to "exist" in any sense that the mind *can* grasp—and of course that *cannot* be said.

In the sixth century, Pseudo-Dionysius suggested that we should engage in a dialectical exercise through which God is called "something" but also "not-something." This exercise should continue through the full range of self-negating dualities—not as an exercise in puerile self-contradiction but as a demonstration of how far beyond our power of comprehension God really is. There is no way possible in which he could constitute a "being" in the same sense that *we* are beings, or that *the cosmos* exemplifies "Being." No, he is something that is totally "other," so we might as well call him "Nothing," disturbing as the gesture may be.

A derivative method was used by the twelfth-century Jewish theologian Rabbi Moses ben Maimon, better known as Moses Maimonides. He bade his followers to approach the understanding of God through the invocation of negative or double-negative attributes—that is, God is "not-imperfect"— as an act of self-disciplined humility to instill in us the realization that our limited minds are incapable of formulating anything at all about God's nature with positive certitude. The very same purpose prompted Meister Eckhart, a fourteenth-century Christian mystic, to say that "God is Nothing."

These formulations compare in some ways—but not in others—to the Buddhist "Sunyata" principle. In Mahayana Buddhism, sunyata ("Void") is an *emptiness* in Dharma, the reality we know, which is devoid of an enduring essence—a complaint that in the Western tradition got its impetus from Plato. The emptiness principle can also apply in a positive sense if applied to Nirvana, the ideal state in which one is free from enslavement to passion and the cycles of reincarnation in which one's karma plays out in successive lives. In this sense, emptiness can mean a liberation from encumbrances.

The "Void" or emptiness doctrine in Buddhism is heavily based in the teachings of Nagarjuna, who lived in the second or third century AD. He proclaimed that our experience is empty—"sunya"—in the sense of lacking a definitive content that lives beyond the flux that we perceive. It is patent enough that phenomena *exist*, but they have no transcendent reality. They are ephemeral and therefore illusory.

They are *empty* of anything that *lasts* in the form of real *Being*.

Sunyata is in no way a doctrine of Nothingness. It is an Asian equivalent of Via Negativa, the Judeo-Christian practice of expressing the ineffable in terms of paradox. Emptiness or Void in the Buddhist tradition is consistent with an acknowledgment of *presence*. This now-you-see-it/now-you-don't ontology is epitomized by the famous saying, "form is emptiness, and emptiness is indeed form" that has circulated in Buddhist culture for centuries. Its source is the "Heart Sutra," a sacred text whose dating and origins are matters of controversy.[10]

So much for "Emptiness." The concept of "Nothingness" must be considered differently.

Poetic license is of course justifiable, and even in everyday usage we employ the word "nothing" in senses that are vague in some respects and yet convey our intended meaning with clarity. "Nothing" is one of those words that at one and the same time (depending on usage) may be cogent in some ways and unintelligible in others. When applied to metaphysics—or even to physics— "nothing" is a term that may be apt and appropriate. Or it may constitute an egregious example of slovenly thinking.

Consider some examples that push the mind to its limits.

We have already distinguished between "nothing" and "emptiness"— understood as a quality of space. But the current theories of physics argue that a *void* cannot exist in "empty space." The physicist Paul Davies points out that when we think that physical space emerged "out of nothing" (ex nihilo) from the Big Bang, we are plunged into conceptual problems in light of the nature of space-time. "The idea of space being created out of nothing," he writes, "is a subtle one that many people find hard to understand, especially if they are used to thinking of space as already being 'nothing.' The physicist, however, regards space as being more like an elastic medium than as emptiness. [...] Because of quantum effects [...] even the purest vacuum is a ferment of activity and is crowded with evanescent structures."[11]

The eminent physicist John Russell Wheeler—who delighted in paradox—used the Via Negativa when he proclaimed with great confidence that the universe indeed came forth ex nihilo and that the cosmos emerged out of "Nothing." "Just as life arose from nonlife on Earth," he wrote, "something arose from nothing in the universe."[12] But the theory of his fellow physicist David Bohm is in most respects better: his theory of a "non-local" implicate order that *contains* the metaphysical potentialities of space and time, "folded up."

Let us now consider the abstraction of "nothing" in its broader significations. Think of it in relation to the question of what, if "anything," may be lurking "outside" of the space-time fabric. We may reply that the answer is "nothing," but what do we mean?

Is there a *negative realm* "surrounding" the fabric—a "Nothingness" strong enough to "hold its own" against Being? Or should Nothing be viewed as just a simple lack of ... "anything"—*zero presence* we will never understand?

The conceptual game goes on and on, and the penchant of the human mind to *visualize* concepts is part of the problem. The situation is sufficiently entertaining to generate literary commentary. John Wilmot, the second Earl of Rochester, penned the following lines in the 1670s:

NOTHING! Thou eldest brother even to Shade,
That hadst a being e'er the world was made ...
Something, the general attribute of all,
Severed from thee, its sole original,
Into thy boundless self must undistinguished fall.[13]

It is hard to avoid giving "nothing" a quality of *presence*. This is surely a commentary on the way the human mind functions.

Consider something else that physics and mathematics teach about a different but related concept: "infinity." There are many different kinds of infinity, and one of them is the principle that things can be infinitely subdivided. Davies puts it this way: "What is the smallest number greater than zero? There is no such number, for every fraction, however small, can always be halved."[14] By the same token, every "moment" in time can be broken down steadily into smaller "moments," and the process can never have an end. For that reason, "any mathematician can demonstrate that there are no more moments in all of eternity than there are in, say, one minute," because both "eternity" and "one minute" have *infinite* moments.

Now apply this principle to "nothing." If we try to probe "downward," can we ever reach a point at which the subdivision stops? The answer is no. We will *never* reach "absolute Nothing."

Or will we?

The question is unanswerable because we have no way of knowing when our concepts apply—or do not apply—to realities that our minds and our senses are powerless to apprehend.

Does *conceptual* subdivision correspond to any *physical* reality? May an infinite series of "presences"—*physical* presences—be lurking in the downward immensity of ... everything? Will a process of *physical* subdivision eventually reach ... nothing?

We don't know.

But even in the point-singularity that numerous physicists regard as the source of the Big Bang—a "point" where space *as such* did not exist—there must have been some sort of "presence."

Or so we think.

But is "presence" just a term that our limited minds cannot fully grasp, even as we think it?

The endless search for nothing has its counterpart in the concept that *Being* never ends. The question as to what exists "outside" the space-time fabric is answered readily by the multiple universe theory. If every possible thing must be happening somewhere, it follows that "outside" our universe are ... others.

Physicist Bryce DeWitt has supported the belief that "every quantum transition taking place on every star, in every galaxy, in every remote corner of the universe is splitting our local world on earth into myriads of copies of itself."[15]

And *where* are these copies of our world? Davies believes they are "very nearby," but they are "inaccessible: we cannot reach them however far we travel through our own space and time." Each of us "is no more than an inch away from millions of his duplicates, but that inch is not measured through the space of our perceptions."[16]

CHAPTER 8

MYSTICISM

Reason and Newton, they are quite two things;
For so the Swallow & the Sparrow sings.
Reason says "Miracle": Newton says "Doubt".
Aye! that's the way to make all Nature out.
"Doubt, doubt, & don't believe without experiment":
That is the very thing that Jesus meant,
When he said, "Only believe! Believe & try!
Try, try, and never mind the Reason why."

WILLIAM BLAKE, *Miscellaneous Epigrams and Fragments*

It is time to give some careful attention to the practices of *mysticism*, for anyone seeking independent spirituality must be tempted at some point or other by the notion that through meditation they can find what they are seeking *directly*.

The workings of our minds are always visceral and emotional as well as cerebral. We use our instincts to make sense of things, and in most cases we are doing this well before we make use of our analytical powers. The practices of mysticism and meditation figure in the history of all the monotheistic religions— especially the traditions of Sufism in Islam and the Kabbalah in Judaism—and Yoga is fundamental to both Hinduism and Buddhism. Many (perhaps most) of the shamanistic religions are grounded in mystical practices.

The link between ultimate reality and human personality is latent in beliefs about "immortal souls"—numinous versions of ourselves that supposedly exist within our mortal bodies. Meditation, ostensibly, deepens the bond with our ethereal self and the ethereal realm from whence it comes.

Small wonder that so many believers have the feeling that by delving into their minds through meditation, they can forge a bond between their innermost identity and the Ultimate. By going inward and downward, they go upward. They *connect* themselves to the force behind everything. Hinduism makes explicit provision for the presence of the ultimate spiritual reality, "Brahman," in all of us via the microcosmic presence of "Atman."

This book has argued that we *are* connected to a higher power through a commonplace phenomenon with vast ontological implications: the experience of *now*. But even if people agree that spirituality is within easy reach in the course of their regular activities, they may go on to ask this question: could meditation *enhance* this kind of spirituality and open up even broader vistas?

There are, of course, different forms of meditation, very different: vipassana meditation is different from transcendental meditation, the version most frequently used for mystical purposes.

Almost all the accounts of mystical meditation tell us that practitioners begin with some repetitive and ritualistic practices to clear the mind of conscious thought as much as possible. Deep breathing and the chanting of a mantra are common examples. As this process takes hold, a feeling of blissful relaxation may ensue. The physiology of this process was analyzed decades ago by Dr. Herbert Benson, a Harvard physician, and Miriam Klipper in their book *The Relaxation Response*, which presented the practices of transcendental meditation for their therapeutic value—for example, in lowering blood pressure.

Mystics have reported that visions may occur in this process. Depending on the repertoire of imagery from different faith traditions to which they are accustomed, they may visualize the Virgin Mary or Hindu "avatars" or Buddha or a wide range of other imagery. From this stage, an "ascent" begins that will waft them into the felt presence of a powerful, beautiful, and indescribable Presence that they take to be Ultimate Reality.

There are many questions to be asked about this practice as a pathway to spirituality, not least of all the question of what this "presence" really *means*. People are always of course quite free to determine what anything *means*, but the challenge of *proving* such meanings will vary depending on the nature of the given experience.

So the question must be asked: have the mystics been brought into contact with something that is *other* than themselves—in a process that overlaps conscious and unconscious mental drives—or have they felt the presence of a thing because they merely *wished* to feel it? In other words, is their experience *really* an encounter with God or an encounter with a dose of pure fantasy? Have they had an experience created by their minds because they *wished* to have it? Is that what it is—and nothing more?

In his account of Eastern mysticism, Fritjof Capra made use of a revealing shortcut that gave away a presupposition. Listen carefully to the following statement: "The direct experience of reality transcends the realm of thought and language, and [...] mysticism is based on such a direct experience."[1] Notice the fact that "reality" is stated in the *singular*, thus implying that mystical experience is *always*—perforce—an encounter with *the one and only* reality. But is it? Everything that we encounter is technically "real" as a matter of pure ontology—it *exists* or *subsists* as a "something"—but *reality in general* will always be encountered by people in a great *plurality of ways*, and some of these encounters will result in ideas that are demonstrably *mistaken* depending on the questions that we ask as we contemplate "reality."

Perhaps these questions don't matter very much—euphoria is what it is, so we might as well enjoy it—but if we stand back from mystical experience and try to make sense of it, it matters, or so it could be argued.

This issue is central to interpretation of "near-death" experiences in which people who are close to death have had experiences that hint at an afterlife: they feel themselves floating as "astral projections" over their bodies, they see a portal of light toward which they are moving, they have visionary revelations, and then they ... "come back to life" and wake up. So what happened?

Sometimes people claim to have witnessed things in their "astral" state that other people later confirm—things that were going on around them as they lay in the grip of a deep coma. It is very difficult to know what to make of these claims. If the evidence is strong, we need to keep an open mind, and yet the startling nature of the claims makes us look at the evidence again and again as we strive to assess its credibility—if we can.

We know from our dreams that the unconscious mind can generate powerful imagery with pictorial content whose clarity can be astonishing, regardless of how incongruous the dream situations may be. The experience of sleep as a familiar mental state can be compared with other states that depart from the normality of wakefulness. Hypnosis is a very good example of a trance state that differs from sleep. And the meditational experience is quite different from hypnosis. A drug-induced psychedelic experience is another "altered state" that is different from sleep.

In the years of the 1960s counterculture, advocates of LSD proposed that drug trips were pathways to "New Age" spirituality and thousands of people accordingly read the books of Carlos Casteneda to learn about shamanistic practices in Mexico that employed the drug mescaline.

Certain trance states are semiconscious, and they can involve appalling behavior. The trance state that apparently occurred in the Sun Dance ritual of the Lakota Sioux involved self-mutilation. Psychiatrists like Erich Fromm have contended that some psychopathic behavior may involve trance states. The Nazi rallies in the 1930s caused a trance state for some of the participants. Those who were swept away by charismatic oratory and the aerobic effects of the repeat-rhythm "Sieg Heil" chant (a mantra) behaved in ways that were at times nothing less than berserk, according to observers. Some American travelers said that the antics they saw in these rallies reminded them of "holy roller" religious services, where believers had convulsions and "spoke in tongues."

In the case of the German women who experienced delirium in response to Hitler's oratory, the sexual dimension of the passing euphoria was obvious. Sexual excitement may involve an element of trance, and its significance depends upon the nature of the sexuality, which can be wholesome or—in the cases of sadism and rape—malignant. Those who experience revelation in a trance may emerge from the experience as charismatic "prophets" who build a mass following around creeds that are demonstrably evil.

History is rife with these dark Messiahs: powerful lunatics who preach liberation through destruction. At their bidding, eruptions of primitivism come from the nameless underground regions that should not be disturbed.

Trance states are serious business.

But the trance states of yoga and related meditational practices are distinctive, insofar as they emphasize a "stillness" and an individual peace that are at odds with the hysteria of charismatic rallies that trigger mass arousal.

In the case of encounters with the "Ultimate" that are described by the mystical practitioners of meditation, the experience of such people will apply in different ways depending on their faith tradition and theology. In the seventeenth century, two radical English Protestant groups took an inward experience of "illumination" and did drastically different things with it: the Quaker experience of "inner light" and the Puritan experience of "conversion" led to opposite social applications of Christianity, one of them extremely tolerant and the other one highly intolerant.

One of the most benign and ecumenical applications of mysticism was the Sufi movement in Islam—as positive and universalistic as the philosophic Falsafah movement that overlapped it in medieval times. One of the most important and useful discourses of Karen Armstrong in recent years has been her effort to bring these traditions to the attention of the world in order to contrast them to the savagery that Islam in its fundamentalist versions has projected for decades. To be sure, the savagery of such fundamentalism has been no worse in some ways than the ferocity of its Christian equivalents. But the blood lust and the sadism of ISIS were a greater menace—for a while, at least—than any other corresponding tyranny in the world.

There were many exemplars of sweetness and light among the Islamic Sufis—many teachers who sought to inculcate love, understanding, and forbearance in the minds of their followers. Among the more influential was the twelfth-century Iranian teacher Yahya Suhrawardi, who blended mysticism, rationality, and philosophic universalism. He taught there are many possible paths in the "search for God."

Another great Islamic teacher in the Sufi tradition was the thirteenth-century mystic Jalal ad-Din Rumi, who is far more widely known to this day by innumerable people as … "Rumi."

It is certainly good to stress the common elements in the experiences of these particular mystics. It is also, however, important to recognize the divergences—in content and outcome—among mystical and prophetic endeavors, some of which can lead to perversion into evil. Mysticism and prophecy can be dangerous, and any quest for a free and independent spirituality grounded in reverence for freedom as a principle must proceed like a bold and yet careful exploration through a minefield.

Like "bad LSD trips," meditational experiences and religious catharsis can turn upon the practitioner. Ignatius Loyola, the founder of the Jesuits, cautioned novices that their devotions might get hijacked by Satan and lead to suicidal depression. Centuries later, during the "Great Awakening" of the 1730s in Puritan New England, hellfire sermons drove some people into such overpowering despair that suicides indeed resulted. The minister Jonathan Edwards, who preached the famous sermon "Sinners in the Hands of an Angry God," attributed these results to Satanic agency.

Those of us who seek the kind of spirituality that balances rationality and passion—one that works for the scientists among us who look upon the miracle of existence with justified wonder—must be working toward a "mystical realism" that is safe and yet provides us with moments that lift us out of a mundane state of mind and take us … higher.

There are several ways to achieve this.

The Hasidic movement in Judaism arose in the eighteenth century. It imbued every moment with a radiant spirituality—a sense of *numinous* quality. If such a mood is hard to sustain for very long, there may still come *extraordinary* moments in life that will bring it forth suddenly.

Scientists have sometimes reported that breakthroughs occur to them as *epiphanies*: inflows of rapid understanding that present the mind with ideas that possess sheer *beauty*. Mathematicians have reported this mental phenomenon: instinctive solutions appear in a flash and then extended computations prove them to be absolutely correct. Einstein reported that his own discoveries occurred in this way and he believed that such experiences should be viewed as essentially spiritual.

Scientists often speak of the "elegance" and "beauty" of the insights that come in such moments, and the *beauty* of the concept is what transfixes them: it fills them with conviction that they are on the right track. Many people in the course of their lives find *aesthetics* to be the best pathway to spirituality.

Aesthetics, of course, can be dangerous in the extreme—if misused by lunatics and killers. The Nazis proved that once and for all, for their "ideals of beauty" were sinister. As always, the pathways to evil are smoothed by seduction, and perversion can feel extremely pleasant.

That said, however, the bond between aesthetics and spirituality is often benign. All around us are examples of the spirituality that people have expressed in inspirational art, music, literature, and architecture.

And religious experience is undeniably quickened if the sudden experience of beauty has a dose of the erotic.

Armstrong has cited the case of the thirteenth-century Sufi teacher Muid ad-Din ibn al-Arabi (often known as Sheikh al-Akbah, the great master), who, in the course of a visit to the Kabah in Mecca, was transfixed by the beauty of a girl—a girl named Nizam. Armstrong compares this to Dante Alighieri's experience, when his encounter with Beatrice—exquisite Beatrice—led him to undertake the meditative and literary quest that would make his name immortal.

Compare it if you wish to the vision of the girl by the sea in the passage from James Joyce's *Portrait*. W. H. Auden has called this experience the "Vision of Eros," an encounter that arouses an erotic response of such artistic power that it ushers in an altered state, a transcendent state: it takes *beauty* and makes it an *epiphany*.

Another way to achieve a state of mystical realism is more intellectual in certain respects but still effective. We can ask ourselves the basic ontological question: why does anything exist instead of nothing, then marvel at the fact that we are here to ask the question at all—alive—in this world. Verse compositions may help, and nearly anyone can make up some lines with resonance:

> There, all round us and within us—
> Quicksilver of the moment we are in
> upholding our existence and being as we
> stay
> fused with the force behind the world in this mysterious
> *Now,*
> Permeating all—
> Force that bears the universe onward to reach itself
> Never.

If words do not come, there is another method that is equally good, if not better. The thing to do is *stand back* from the immediacy that you feel, the *awareness* you have of *being here this very instant*, and use the Via Negativa. Think something along these lines: wait a minute, none of this makes any real sense if you stop to think about it, nothing accounts for the fact that I or anything else that I see and feel should be here at all, there is in fact *no need* for me or anything else to be here, and yet we *are*.

We just *are*, in an arbitrary outburst of *freedom* that *calls* the whole thing into being and *supports* it every moment through a never-absent and always subsisting *guarantee of being-ness*, a *power* that we designate *now*, for lack of any better word. What is it? What it *feels* like (to use some visual language) is a pure *liquid clarity* that constitutes the *medium* in which we live and move and have our being. It carries us along and makes us part of a moving *point of focus* that *defines* or *presents* or *expresses* what the universe *is*—and does—every moment. That's what it is.

Try that.

Of course we have to remember that ventures in ontology like that are just visualizations (like Heidegger's metaphors of "falling" and being "thrown") that are limited *perceptions* of things we will never really grasp. The terms "liquid clarity" and "focus" are nothing more than handy visualizations that would surely break down under deeper analysis—if our minds were only capable of such analysis.

Still, every moment you experience awareness and gaze upon the world you have a revelation—nothing less—if you take it that way, and you should if you are *seeking* revelation. Your own existence every moment is *direct revelation*: it reveals *in immediate terms* a transcendent and immanent power, the power of Being as it moves in Becoming, and nothing we know can account for it.

In recent decades, some writers on spirituality have striven, with varying degrees of success, to use quantum mechanics and its deeper implications to create a kind of cosmological *creed*. These people are on the right track, and their efforts are clearly germane to the purpose of this book.

Indeed, I include myself among them to a certain extent, for the affinities between us are clear.

All of us—in our very different ways—are part of a tradition that is centuries-old. We are seeking not only to reconcile the ways of science and spirituality but to find a *new* spirituality in science. We have a great deal in common, but we definitely think for ourselves. So I will quickly explain where I differ from some of the other people who have sought to "find God in the new physics."

I find some of their theories naïve. Their enthusiasm tends to run wild—and it leads to dubious notions.

Many of these writers have embraced the idea of pan-psychism in light what we know about quantum mechanics, and their ruminations are at times very interesting and cogent. They often speak of the cosmos as something of a *dream* with ourselves as participatory dreamers.

That's a potent idea—in certain ways. Even so, they take a very wrong turn in their tendency to make strong claims without reliable evidence.

They create metaphysical doctrines that are fraught with so many contradictions that they make no sense. They engage in assertions regarding things they merely *wish* to be true. Some, for example, have insisted on the doctrine of human immortality—as an article of pure *belief*—with nothing but a happy leap of faith to back them up. And wishful thinking never carries an argument.

Others invoke the "observer principle" of quantum mechanics—the fact that particles in countless experiments have changed their behavior under human observation—to say that we can "dream" the universe into improvement or give the world some sort of a utopian peace, and such claims are of course very weak: they do not stand up under scrutiny. *Freedom* in the cosmos appears to be real, and yet the task of finding ways to *project* it—to make *use* of it—is tricky. Those who believe that meditation or deliberative dreaming can alter the world must offer proof; they must show us what their methods can do.

The problem of evil is predictably neglected in many of these theories. Or it is treated in a formulaic manner. In short, these well-intentioned productions are often disappointing, for all their sincerity. So what these writers ought to do is take a good hard look at their doctrines, reflect, and try again, for they are on the right track.[2]

Still another path to mystical realism seems to be largely intellectual, but it can waft the mind into a meditational state through the magic of Via Negativa.

Different practices were developed in the Chinese and Japanese versions of Zen Buddhism to induce a contemplative state by focusing one by one *and then collectively all at once* on one's own inner functions. After that, the initiates try to transcend these inner states—float above them—dismissing them "as though" they were "emptiness." A more ambitious technique is to contemplate *the full totality of everything there is,* and then levitate *as though it were emptiness.* The continuum of self-negating wholeness and emptiness may coax the mind into a state of calm equilibrium, approaching what might be considered a foretaste of Nirvana.

Pseudo-Dionysisus and Moses Maimonides played upon a comparable dialectic—or mental game—in the contemplation of monotheistic divinity: God could be said to be "Something" and yet "Not-Something," presence and absence, a subsistent ineffability the contemplation of which may bring wonder to the mind of the believer—a calmness verging into ecstasy or something very like it.

Modern physics permits us to do something similar if we contemplate the "singularity"—the one from which the Big Bang supposedly arose. Scientists are still debating whether a Bang from a "hot singularity" accounts for the cosmos. But the concept of Bang still possesses enough cogency for present purposes.

Thirty years ago, Paul Davies—physicist commentator and spiritual seeker— discoursed on the nature of the cosmic singularity in his book *God and the New Physics*. He made use of the Via Negativa, the practice that many theologians call the "apophatic" method: defining things by what they are *not*.

Recall the paradox: for the universe to be *caused* or *created*, an event must occur within a process of before-and-after that we understand as time. Space-time was *absent* in the point-singularity—or so we are told—and yet the Bang in some manner we can never understand just *emerged from it*. Hence the paradox: how could the Bang or anything like it transpire without temporal causation? The best that the physicists can do—the ones who subscribe to the Big Bang theory— is argue that "quantum fluctuations" must account for the mystery.

And yet the mystery continues: *why* are there quantum fluctuations?

"Space and time," wrote Davies, "could have sprung into existence spontaneously without violating the laws of physics." Indeed, "space-time could pop out of nothingness as the result of a causeless quantum transition."[3] A causeless quantum transition … emergence out of nothing … a process consistent with "the laws of physics," however unexplainable the process may be. But this begs an obvious question: Where did the laws of physics come from? Out of nothing? Or out of something?

Fritjof Capra pointed out the parallel between the paradoxes of the "new physics" and the "*koans*"—the mind-challenging riddles that address the ineffable through conceptual poetry—in Zen Buddhism, and the application to the cosmological riddle is especially relevant.

Davies began his ruminations on the point-singularity in a pointedly apophatic manner, and here is what he said: "A singularity is most certainly not a thing. It is the boundary of a thing (spacetime)."[4] This leads to a case of Zen-like paradox, because "thing" connotes a concept that the human mind uses—loosely, to be sure—as an "object" for contemplation and limited analysis. The point-singularity is surely a concept that human minds produced, and thus *a thing* at least in that sense.

But it is *not* a thing, according to Davies, and that's *wonderful* for mystical uses. Davies continues: "Because all our physical theories so far are formulated in the context of space and time, the existence of a boundary to spacetime suggests that natural physical processes cannot be continued beyond such a thing." Point duly noted: we are discussing a *thing*.

Regardless, "in a fundamental sense a singularity represents, according to this view, the outer limits of the natural universe." It also represents the limits of what the mind can conceptualize and what human language can express. He continued: "at a singularity, matter may enter or leave the physical world, and influences may emanate therefrom that are totally beyond the power of physical science to predict, even in principle. A singularity is the nearest *thing* [emphasis added] that science has found to a supernatural agent."[5]

Perfect: a thing/not-thing that even science may regard as a supernatural agent. Contemplate that the next time your moods lead you to ask the ontological question: Why does anything exist instead of nothing?

CHAPTER 9

A PATH OF ONE'S OWN

The religious situation in many parts of the world at this writing is very bleak by the standards of independent spirituality.

Fundamentalism (as usual) is a force of wicked persecution and oppression. Christianity and Islam have been especially hard-hit by the scourge. The commentary to follow is as harsh as I can make it, since the plague of fundamentalism is not only an affront to common decency, it is also a danger—a threat—that can blight people's lives without warning.

FUNDAMENTALIST SAVAGERY

Evangelicals send their children to indoctrination camps they call "schools" for systematic brainwashing, and "Islamists" seek to "radicalize" potential converts in such a way as to elicit their potential for committing atrocities.

They fan out across the world to commit these atrocities in the guise of what some continue to call "terrorism," a grotesquely euphemistic term—"terrorist" is only slightly less insipid as a descriptive term than "militant"—that conceals the real truth about these people—namely, they are psychopathic death-worshippers and necrophiles.

Imagine the act of driving a van down a road by the beach and then mowing down dozens of men, women, and children. This was actually done in France. Imagine breaking into a Christmas party with an assault rifle and turning dozens of happy people into bloody corpses. This was actually done in San Diego. The obscenity of these acts is beyond the power of words to express and they were done as acts of … religious devotion.

Acts of worship.

All the while, the ruthless application of Shariah law in a number of countries—especially Iran and Saudi Arabia—denies millions the right to determine what kind of a life they choose to live, and the degradation of women in these countries is nothing less than shameful.

America—land of the free—had its moral values perverted systematically in 2016 and afterward by evangelicals who strive to make America the land of the unfree. They demonstrated their true moral values through their fervent support for a moral degenerate, Donald Trump. Perhaps some of them chose to *overlook* the coarseness and indecency of Trump, but others—at least to judge them by their own recorded words—*loved it*. They *admired* the way that Trump systematically dominated, humiliated, and ridiculed the weak. This flattered the prideful and vainglorious evangelical conceit that they are God's "elect" and that the misfortunes of others must be meted out by Providence to *sinners* who *deserve* the misfortunes.

So when Trump ridiculed the victims of a hurricane in Puerto Rico, he did it with the whole-hearted approval of his vicious "base." The same thing occurred when he separated children from their parents and locked them up in cages in the desert because their parents were desperate refugees—people seeking the American dream but instead receiving the Christian charity of evangelicals in the form of belligerence.

"Christians," these people call themselves.

No act of cruelty is beyond their contemplation, so long as they justify it to themselves by invoking the *one single issue* they use to prove (to their own satisfaction) their own righteousness: the issue of *abortion*. As long as one is "pro-life" by their standards, one can perpetrate any act of desecration—any violation of the Sermon on the Mount—that springs to mind. Like Milton's Satan, the motto of these people would appear to be "Evil, be thou my good," just as long as they remain "pro-life."

They say they champion the "rights of the unborn," and this formulation permits them to define the termination of *any* pregnancy as murder—even a pregnancy that has formed just a split-second after a sperm has fertilized an egg, or a pregnancy that results from an act of rape or incest. They do this based upon a "faith" supposition that a pregnancy embodies an "immortal soul"—whether a soul that has preexisted "from eternity" or one that has been freshly created and placed within the newly formed fetus they seldom bother to say. This is a dogmatic assertion that is absolutely beyond the power of anyone to prove.

But they couldn't care less. It's good enough for them, because this is after all a matter of "faith."

"Faith."

The vainglorious pretension of these people is symptomatic of a very deep moral perversion. Their Christian love (so-called) is directed single-mindedly toward "the unborn" while they treat *the living* with hatred as they seek symbolic victims to persecute. It is entirely possible that the age-old Christian belief that the act of sex transmits and embodies "original sin"—a doctrine emerging in part from Saint Augustine, with his teaching that worldly "concupiscence" exemplifies contempt for godly purity—is the driving force behind the evangelical obsession with the issue of abortion. After all, this is a matter of *sex.*

Unwanted pregnancies in the evangelical view must perforce result from *sinful sex* that deserves to be *punished,* as long as that punishment is inflicted on a *woman.* Defense of the unborn permits these people to indulge (indirectly and through hints) in their shameful and prurient fascination with the sex lives of other people.

The persecution of women who seek alternatives to unwanted pregnancy might well be regarded as a latter-day counterpart to the "witch craze" that terrorized Europe in the sixteenth and seventeenth centuries. In the search for "demonic" activity among their victims, inquisitors unleashed a demonic rage of their own, thus demonstrating what mental health practitioners call "projection:" imputing their own beastliness to their victims. You take the evil in yourself and then project it to your victims, thus transforming every vile act of your own into a victory for justice.

The mental tyranny of Christian fundamentalism has been made explicit by the "Christian Reconstruction" or "Dominion" movement, which has sought to turn the United States into an explicit theocracy. A key figure in the movement was the late Rousas John Rushdoony, a Calvinist who made war upon independent thinking. "All non-Christian knowledge is sinful, invalid nonsense," he declared, and any attempt by people to think for themselves is "to set up another God in contempt of the LORD."[1]

He attacked public schools because they give children access to ideas outside of the Bible, whose teachings must be forced upon everyone. "The fundamental task of Christian education," he wrote, is "subduing the earth," and "in every way asserting the crown rights of King Jesus in every realm of life."[2] Biblical law (as interpreted by him) must replace any other law. "Theonomy" was what he called his social vision—from "nomos," the Greek word for law.

Dominion, subjugation, and control formed the basis for Rushdoony's Christianity, and mind-control as well as violence were to be used against any who resist. Rushdoony supported the death penalty for (among many others) homosexuals, adulterers, and those who lie about their virginity. He enthusiastically invoked the principle of top-down hierarchy, proclaiming that "some people are by nature slaves."[3]

A charming fellow, was he not? Fortunately for the contemporary world, this Christo-fascist passed away in 2001, but his mind-enslaving followers abound. Margaret Atwood's nightmarish novel *The Handmaid's Tale* (1985) was written in part as a response to the demand of the Christian far-right for a new social order based upon the harsh strictures of "theonomy." The novel depicts a fanatical movement whose "faith" gives perverts a made-to-order excuse for the sexual subjugation of women. This dystopian fantasy is convincing, for the appetites of tyranny are boundless and the people who excel in the art of cloaking sick desires in the trappings of righteousness are never in short supply.

So much for fundamentalism, a disease of contemporary times that will never be eradicated by reason, compassion, and mercy. The Christian variation of the scourge is powerful because of a distinctive quality in the culture of Christianity itself: a schizoid quality deriving from Saint John, who took the Jesus of the first three Gospels—the Jesus of meekness and love and humility—and made him also the imperious bane of all "children of the devil," the implacable judge who will mete out damnation on Judgment Day. Hence the split between the side of Christianity that holds out the prospect of universal mercy and the side that threatens anyone who chooses to embrace any other form of mercy. This makes Christianity—*in the wrong hands*—one of the cruelest religions that ever existed, and this situation will continue despite all the efforts to *transform* the faith as it has been transformed so many times by forceful theologians and their followers.

My indictment of evangelical fundamentalism is largely applicable to Protestant behavior, but reform of the Catholic Church remains, as ever, an enormous uphill battle for Catholic believers in freedom who decide to remain Roman Catholics. The Catholic position on abortion is substantially the same as the Protestant fundamentalist position, and the task of changing Catholic teachings is a matter of challenging not only papal authority but the authority of the entire ecclesiastical hierarchy.

MAINSTREAM RELIGION AND NONCONFORMITY

These complaints present a one-sided version of the world situation when it comes to religion. Billions of decent and compassionate people find comfort in religious traditions that affirm the very best of human nature. They embrace the traditions in which they were raised, and these traditions are valuable to them. The rituals they practice give them comfort as they seek to experience authentic spirituality—to fulfill a human longing that most of us instinctively feel.

But there comes a time in the life of a great many people when they start to feel a restlessness that disturbs their religious routine—a time when they begin to feel that something is *missing* in the way that they practice religion.

They become *"seekers."* They may decide to experiment, to sample and evaluate other doctrines—other methods. Some become converts and others turn to mysticism in one form or another. Karen Armstrong endeavored in the 1990s to emphasize the wholesomeness of mystical paths as opposed to fundamentalism. She emphasized the decency of the Sufi tradition and compared it to the loving side of Christian piety as exemplified in the life of Saint Francis of Assisi.

Particularly edifying for readers both in Christendom and in the world of Islam were her accounts of the Sufis who advocated freedom, who insisted that every single person in the world is—at least in some sense—an avatar of God, wherefore we should practice toleration and empathy when it comes to creedal differences between religions.

In my preface, I spoke about the *limits* of toleration when it comes to creeds that generate tyranny. My harsh view of fundamentalism illustrates the point. The problem of evil is real, and we must confront it sometimes if we encounter oppressive behavior. But evil is protean and we ourselves may succumb. Fundamentalists (grudgingly) agree with this, but only in the childish and superstitious way that their faith permits. They hail the "amazing grace" that saves "wretches" like themselves, but with "grace" (whatever that means) they feel so exalted—not wretched—that their sense of infallible and imperious certitude never abates.

For this is "faith."

They let their creed do their thinking for them as they face the complexities of life with slogans. Any real *analysis* of their own situation is beyond them.

But there will never be a substitute for thinking things through, and a whole *way of life* should be built around the practice. Julia Sweeney, in her rejection of organized religion, argued that if God exists, he ought to *want* her to use the brains she has.

Armstrong shared with her readers vivid samples of the anger—and its justifications—that led her to rebel. "Once the Bible begins to be interpreted literally instead of symbolically," she wrote, "the idea of God becomes impossible. To imagine a deity who is literally responsible for everything that happens on earth involves impossible contradictions. The 'God' of the Bible ceases to be a symbol of a transcendent reality and becomes a cruel and despotic tyrant."[4]

Perhaps the last straw for her was the way in which Milton's *Paradise Lost* presented God the Father in a way that struck her as vacuous: God tries to rationalize his own providence in "lengthy conversations of deep tedium" with God the Son. Armstrong: "God comes across as callous, self-righteous and entirely lacking in the compassion that his religion was supposed to inspire."[5]

She thought about "the cruelty of so much Christian history."[6] She thought about the way that "people died as martyrs for holding views that it was impossible to prove one way or the other."[7] So she came to her own conditional conclusion, framed as a question: "Could it be that a deliberately imaginative conception of God, based on mythology and mysticism, is more effective as a means of giving his people courage to survive tragedy and distress than a God whose myths are interpreted literally?"[8]

Not only was the God of Christian tradition "cold and legalistic, he is also grossly incompetent," she said. As God drones on in Milton's poem with his justification of the plan he set in motion before history started, "it occurs to the reader that there must have been an easier and more direct way to redeem mankind. The fact that the tortuous plan with its constant failures and false starts is decreed in advance can only cast grave doubts on the intelligence of its Author."[9]

At last, years of pent-up denial found joyous release for Armstrong in rebellion, and she said so triumphantly. Anyone who prizes and loves their own God-given freedom must smile as they read this proclamation:

> It is wonderful not to have to cower before a vengeful deity, who threatens us with eternal damnation if we do not abide by his rules. We have a new intellectual freedom and can boldly follow up our own ideas without pussyfooting around difficult articles of faith, feeling all the while a sinking loss of integrity.[10]

Peoples' sensibilities are endlessly different, and mundane religious practices, rituals, and rules can bring priceless inspiration and comfort. The meditational practices of mysticism can also be uplifting—if practiced with care—for those who cultivate the right state of mind and become connoisseurs of the art.

But for those of us who seek their own form of realistic and wide-awake spirituality, there are ways for us to cultivate a true sense of wonder that becomes absolutely spontaneous. If we condition our minds to appreciate the miracle of existence and cease our habitual practice of taking it for granted, the spirituality of life may become, in the felicitous phrase of Mr. Jefferson, self-evident.

This conception is in some respects equivalent to *Zen*, which strives to fill every moment with wonder. But *realistic* mysticism must include the higher mental process—the process that incorporates critical analysis—that is missing from the practices of Zen, which uses paradox to *stifle* analysis.

Paradox is often interesting and very enlightening—but it should never stop intellectuality.

A better Asian grounding for a wide-awake spirituality was developed by the sage Chang Tsai (or Zhang Zai) in the eleventh century. His approach remains interesting and useful. He saw the force behind the universe as "chi," which is widely understood within Chinese tradition as a vital essence. Many have learned about "chi" through the applications of Chinese medicine like acupuncture.

But Chang Tsai took the concept further. He saw "chi" as a much larger force—the source of existence. "Chi" in this sense may be plausibly compared to what we feel when we experience *now*. It is *immediate*, immanent, and *with us*. It is macrocosmic and omnipresent in its scope.

Every instant we can *feel* it.

If Chang Tsai was correct, then the Buddhists may very well be wrong: our lives are not *maya* (illusion) but *chi*. We are not insubstantial, we are *real* participants in *wonder*. We are *physical events* that have reality as sovereign existents—organic productions of Being as it moves in Becoming.

Years ago, the theologian Paul Tillich made significant use of ontology in his magnum opus, the three-volume work *Systematic Theology*. Though his theology embodied the standard apologetics of Christian orthodoxy that independent-minded people will reject, he did approach the subject in a way that was in tune with the scientific discoveries that were already emergent by the time he passed away in 1965.

He defined God as the Ground of Being. And no better definition of divinity could be offered in light of what we know about the universe and its workings. Moreover, this formulation was not without precedent: in the early Middle Ages Duns Scotus Erigena concluded that God is "greater than Being."

Greater than Being.

An important distinction because, in their quest to explore the ineffable, metaphysicians from the time of Parmenides onward spoke of "Being" as a sovereign principle, transcendent and immanent, while theologians from the Middle Ages on, in their quest to express the ineffability of God, sometimes called him "Nothing" in the hope of suggesting that he has to be completely different from any possible "thing" that our experience permits us to grasp. "Nothing," that is, no-*Thing*.

But to call God the "Ground of Being" is better—better because it avoids the inherent clumsiness of the "Nothing" formulation while exploring the idea that a dimension higher than "Being" itself can be conceived.

In its own strange way, no concept could be more bracing—even thrilling—than this as a spur to metaphysical speculation. Armstrong notes that "participation in such a God above 'God' does not alienate us from the world but immerses us in reality. It returns us to ourselves."[11]

Why does anything exist instead of nothing? Let us go on asking that question every day as we look all around us and inward at the gorgeous dispensation.

TOWARD A NEW ENLIGHTENMENT

By my own standards, the intellectual culture of the eighteenth-century Enlightenment deserves to be revived on a very large scale. Its emphasis on the *freedom* of people to rid themselves of superstition and open their minds to discoveries of science remains as valid as ever. It is *of greater importance than ever* in today's morbid world—a world in which unreason and rant are driving hordes of troubled people to commit the most hideous of crimes every day.

Armstrong, so much a champion of the free and dispassionate critique of all spiritual orthodoxies, critiques the Enlightenment as well because in her opinion its emphasis on rationality went overboard and discounted the *mysteries* that ought to be explored through a vigorous and creative exercise of the *imagination*—even to the point of creative myth-making. But mysticism and myth have distinctive dangers, the presentation of which at this point would be redundant.

Armstrong herself acknowledged that "mysticism-for-everybody" can be "dangerous," that mystics themselves often "stressed the perils of the spiritual paths and warned against hysteria," that "Born-Again Christianity" in particular can lead to "frenzied behavior."[12]

So is science the alternative?

Davies the physicist has thought long and hard about the volatile and contradictory significance that religion and science continue to have for billions of people. He made generalizations back in the 1980s—some of them excessively broad, but almost all of them partially true.

Due to the *usefulness* of science, he wrote, "most of our institutions are organized pragmatically, with religion, insomuch as it is included at all, relegated to a stylized role."[13] Of course, this generalization applies much more to the democracies than to theocracies, like that of Iran.

Among sophisticates, there is a "huge disaffection with established religion," not least of all due to its ever-active inclination to dominate, dictate, and persecute.[14] Even so, we live in a world "that, in spite of appearances, is still fundamentally religious."[15] Spirituality of some sort is predictable.

It is telling that "the rise of the new physics has been accompanied by a tremendous growth of interest concerning the deeper philosophical implications of science."[16] This fuses with tradition sometimes, for a great many people who pray to a personal God find it handy to blame life's catastrophes on … "Mother Nature." Such *dualism* may be common all over the world.

In the recent past certain writers tried to argue that science "disproves" religion. Their polemics were foolish in light of the many contributions that physicists have made down the years as spiritual seekers—and even on occasion as mystics. Among the influential "science-versus-religion" books of recent years are *The God Delusion* by Richard Dawkins, *God Is Not Great: How Religion Poisons Everything* by Christopher Hitchens, and *God, the Failed Hypothesis: How Science Shows God Does Not Exist* by Victor Stenger.

The contempt of these people for *organized* religion is quite understandable—and often valid. But their dogmatic assertions on matters metaphysical are nothing less than *pseudo*-scientific. If they had limited their scorn to the weaknesses of organized religion, their assertions would be stronger. But that is not what these writers chose to do.

For centuries, prominent scientists have been drawn by inexorable force to the broader implications of what they were studying. And their ruminations led them quickly to the problems of spirituality. Isaac Newton provides a good example. He had nothing but contempt for the myth-based superstitions of Christianity, but he felt driven to imbue the cosmic principles whose mathematical basis he was explicating with numinous power. And he engaged in explicit theological speculation centered on the doctrine of divine emanation.

John Maynard Keynes—famed for his work as an economist but gifted with a wide-ranging intellect that made him a prominent member of the "Bloomsbury" literary circle—was fascinated the spirituality of Newton. He delivered a lecture on the subject in 1942 that was published just after his death. His reflections make interesting reading. All of Newton's "unpublished works on esoteric and theological matters," wrote Keynes, "are marked by careful learning," and the best of them "are just as sane as the *Principia*, if their whole matter and purpose were not magical." Keynes went on as follows:

> Why do I call him a magician? Because he looked on the whole universe and all that is in it *as a riddle*, a secret which could be read by applying pure thought to certain evidence, certain mystic clues which God had laid about

the world to allow a sort of philosopher's treasure hunt to the esoteric brotherhood.[17]

This instinct—especially among the physicists and mathematicians—was given a new lease on life in the twentieth century by the revolutionary impact of relativity theory and quantum mechanics. Einstein regarded his findings as imbued with spiritual meaning, as did Niels Bohr and other pioneers of quantum theory.

Physicist and science writer Chet Raymo observes that "the mystic and the scientist have this in common: they seek the same deeply hidden essence of creation, and both are, by and large, content that much of what they seek remains unknown. Mystic and scientist live at the portal between knowledge and mystery."[18] Raymo characterizes himself as a "religious naturalist."

God and the New Physics was the title that was given by Paul Davies to one of his most influential books, and the trend that his prominent participation exemplified was both predictable and natural.

As a scientist, Davies shared the not-surprising conviction that "advances in fundamental science are more likely to reveal the deeper meaning of existence than appeal to traditional religion." He even said that science may probably offer "a surer path to God than religion."[19] But the search for a "path to God" is most certainly—indeed by definition—a matter of religion.

Science and religion should not be viewed as mutually exclusive. Science takes the lead, but the spontaneous speculations of independent-minded people will necessarily follow. The kind of spirituality that could usher in a new and much-needed Enlightenment must take its cues from scientific findings, but what are we to *make* of those findings?

What do they *mean* if applied to the questions as to *why* the cosmos exists and what existence implies?

Our minds as they are currently configured reach an impasse when it comes to these questions. We sketch the outer limits of the mystery, but the power to penetrate the mystery eludes us. We can go *just so far* when it comes to matters of religion—and no farther.

But the exercise of thinking through the issues may contribute in a small way to progress. The current findings of brain physiology show that the more we put our minds to vigorous use, the more powerful our minds become. Connectivity of neurons increases as we challenge our minds to do more.

So perhaps this question should be asked: if enough people practice independent spirituality, will their activity lead over time—perhaps a great deal of time, perhaps thousands of years—to a *quantum leap* in the evolution of the human species? Who can say? Prehistoric humans were surely incapable of thinking with anything close to the sophistication that is possible today and the cranial capacity of *Homo sapiens* increased with evolution of the species, according to the paleontologists.

Evolution accelerates via quantum leaps that are called mutations—and mutations seem to be related to quantum fluctuations.

So if we push our minds harder as we go about living and encourage our descendants to carry on the work, who can say what the human mind will be able to see and comprehend long after we are gone?

CHAPTER 10

ONTOLOGY AND MIND

Whatever the truth about divinity, our religious experience is *mental*. O*nly* in our minds and through our minds can we experience anything and that will always be the way that things are. The mind is a metaphysical mystery that continues to perplex philosophers and scientists. Some believe that the existence of mind is a clue that can help us explore the nature of the cosmos.

Quantum mechanics has shown that the observation of subatomic particles affects their movement. This situation is beyond the power of science to understand—at least to date—and we may never understand it. While it sounds unbelievable, controlled experiments have confirmed it again and again.

So what does it mean? We don't know—at least not yet.

But it hints at one of several ways in which mind can affect reality through channels that are deeply mysterious. A related problem is the nature of the mind–brain–body relations that we experience but cannot yet fully explain.

"Materialists" once held that the mind is an "epiphenomenon"—that awareness is nothing but an emanation that emerges somehow from the physical and biological processes taking place "below." It is interesting to note that while physicists were quick to acknowledge nonlinear events as the findings of quantum mechanics revealed them, the life sciences for many years were stubbornly mechanistic, with a linear view of cause and effect that dismissed the idea that a "life force" as such exists.

The doctrine of a "life force" was once known as "vitalism" and the field of biology dismissed it as an odd and discredited doctrine until very recently. There is still a strong tendency in the field of brain physiology to regard our sense of free will as a subjective *sensation* that is caused by the chain reactions of neurons. At this writing, however, that view is being questioned in the rapidly emerging field of *quantum biology*.

Back in 1979, a scholar of cognitive science named Douglas Hofstadter caused a stir with his book *Gödel, Escher, Bach: An Eternal Golden Braid*. His argument was grounded in an emergent movement for "holistic" studies. As opposed to "reductionism," which seeks scientific explanations through analysis of substructures—by breaking phenomena down into smaller and smaller constituent parts that may emanate "upward" in chain reactions—"holism" studies the way in which systems reach a critical mass that can take on "*a life of its own*" and thus achieve a kind of self-referent identity that transcends its constituent parts.

One of Hofstadter's best examples was the ant colony: a community of ants creates elaborate and systematic structures in a way that goes far beyond what any individual ant or even small groups of ants could presumably "invent." And the analogy to the human mind suggests itself: though our awareness is *grounded* in the action of neurons "down below" in the brain, once a critical mass of such action is achieved, a holistic reality takes shape that achieves a life of its own and develops its own distinct patterns—its own distinct "rules" that transcend the actions of the neurons.

The essentials were introduced as early as 1925 by the philosopher C. D. Broad in his book *The Mind and Its Place in Nature*, with its commentary on "emergence." Mind *emerges*, he wrote, when the neurophysiological processes reach a critical mass of complexity, and this aggregate achieves properties beyond what is present in the parts of the brain that gave it birth.

The *location* of this realm is an issue that surpasses our current powers of understanding. Though common sense presumes that mind is "in the brain," it may *transcend* the structure of space-time in ways we can never comprehend.[1]

In this model, both the truth of the reductionist method and the truth of holistic studies are real—and though they clearly relate to each other through cause and effect, the big holistic reality *goes on* to achieve a transcendent and autonomous state that is to some extent *distinct* from the reductionist base that supports it.

Then the story gets mystical, for at times a "Strange Loop," as Hofstadter calls it, is created, and the higher level, though it emanates in part from the lower level, reaches down and reciprocally *affects* the lower level—affects it and changes it. And this suggests that the sense of awareness in our minds, though it springs from neural activity in our brains, will achieve a life of its own from which volition arises: our minds decide that we should *do something*—get up and take a walk, for example—so our minds *command* the neurons to initiate the action in our arms and our legs and our torsos. Hofstadter put the matter this way:

My belief is that the explanations of "emergent" phenomena in our brains—for instance, ideas, hopes, images, analogies, and finally consciousness and free will—are based in a kind of Strange Loop, an interaction between levels in which the top level reaches back down toward the bottom level and influences it, while at the same time being determined by the bottom level. [...] The self comes into being the moment it has the power to reflect itself.[2]

If this theory is true, it may account for something even stranger that many philosophers have studied: the way that our sense of awareness has the power to "step back from itself," in a very odd manner. Consider this example: I know that I am writing this sentence, and a part of this knowledge is the fact that I can *think about* the way that I am writing this sentence as I write it. Indeed, I can critique the very nature of my thoughts at the moment I am thinking them. But in order to do this, a kind of higher "dimension" of myself must "step back" from my busy working self so it can ponder and evaluate its work. And all this can take place *simultaneously*.

To vary the imagery, my consciousness and thus my selfhood soar "upward" level by level, to look down upon—and even influence—the self-analysis that is taking place "below." At the very same time that I think about my very own existence, I can take a step away from the thought and behold myself thinking it from a higher vantage point of selfhood.

In other words, I *know* that I have a self-conscious identity, and furthermore I *know that I know*, and while we're on that particular subject, I *know that I know that I know*.

Psychiatrist Paul R. Fleishman gives another example: "As we try to understand the world and the wonder it creates in us, we come back to the nature of our own wondering mind, and wonder about it."[3]

So what is going on as this happens?

The problem could be viewed as something of an "infinite regress," but a better way to think of it is infinite progress—as my self-awareness, my selfhood, soars further and further "aloft."

In the 1920s, a precocious aeronautical engineer named John William Dunne fantasized that our "ultimate self" is a supernatural "animus" that gazes down upon the "lower" simultaneous iterations of itself as they subsist in different time dimensions. Every mental field of presentation looks down upon the one just below it, and so on. He called this theory "Serialism," and his observations had an element of cogency. He put it this way:

How would you define rationally a "self-conscious" observer—define him so as to distinguish him from a non-self-conscious recorder such as a camera? You should begin, I imagine, by enunciating the truism that the individual in question must be […] able to say: This is *my*-"self." And that means that he must be aware of a "*self*" *owning the* "*self*" *first considered*. Recognition of this second "self" involves, for similar reasons, knowledge of a third "self"—and so on, ad infinitum.[4]

Dunne's theory of "Serialism," as grounded in the doctrine of multidimensional time, is just a theory, but it shows the way that our creative minds are stimulated by the contemplation and analysis of their own inner workings.

Back to the simpler and far more credible version of multilevel mental activity: the "Strange Loop" of Hofstadter, through which the spontaneous actions of holistic mind affect the physical process in which they are based.

Enter quantum mechanics, for a number of theoreticians have concluded that spontaneous mental activity may be a quantum state, that is, it may be grounded in the way that elementary particles can move "without cause."[5] This proposition is highly controversial, and while some physicists resist or deride it, others, such as Roger Penrose and Henry P. Stapp, have enthusiastically supported it.

Physicist Freeman Dyson once wrote that "our consciousness is not just a passive epiphenomenon carried along by the chemical events in our brains, but is an active agent forcing the molecular complexes to make choices between one quantum state and another."[6] "Make choices." It is not surprising that the quantum biologists are coming to believe that the "willful" quanta *act together* in patterns of coherent orchestration, not only in the biological scope of every organism but throughout the biosphere.

Biologist Harold Morowitz believes that "emergence" goes far beyond the life sciences. "Several physicists and philosophers of science," he writes, "detect a kind of noetic feature deep in physics."[7] "Noesis" is *knowing*, and Morowitz made this observation in a book about science and religion.

Henry P. Stapp believes that the dipolar structure attributed by Whitehead to "actual occasions" has validity. He has even developed a new and innovative way to merge Whitehead's ontology with quantum theory. Adopting Whitehead's terms, he speculates that "every Whiteheadian actual occasion/entity has a 'mental pole and a 'physical pole.' "[8]

Here again is pan-psychism, that perennial theory that is one of the inevitable creations of the human mind. We may never be able to *confirm* this theory, and plenty of philosophers and scientists have called it absurd.

But that has not stopped the speculation, for an obvious reason: the skeptics in this case *don't know* the real truth—nobody does—for which reason they ought to be more prudent before rushing into these sorts of speculative matters with dogmatic certitude.

And the same thing applies to philosophers and physicists who subscribe to the doctrine of "block time." It is time to take another hard look at this doctrine and subject it to very close scrutiny. In the context of what we have been saying, the reason should be obvious: themes of *mind*—freedom, becoming, volition, spontaneity, and power in the medium of *now*—become meaningless if time is an illusion. Our experience of life is incoherent and drained of all substance if time is an illusion.

Let us therefore return to the very strange world of the people who insist upon "block time."

This review will itself take some time.

"Emergence" is one of the most exciting and popular issues across the disciplines today. Studies of emergence are fraught with excitement because of their *applicability*, which derives from our experience. And our experience is based upon the clear proposition that change and the time-flow are real.

Block-time theory, by contrast, is intellectually dead except for its residual power to provoke. It has no other *applications*, though philosophers and scientists will sometimes acknowledge it with reverence.

Should they?

Or should they view it as merely a sad demonstration of the mind's capacity to mislead itself? *For this too is a potentiality of mind* that is worthy of study.

We are justified in making some demands of the block-time people. Let them give a clear account of their hypothesis. Let us put them on the spot and make them tell us what their theory really *means*.

As previously noted, the doctrine that time is an illusion goes all the way back to Parmenides, and modern philosophers have sometimes enthusiastically embraced it. "Eternalism" is the term that ontologists have given to this sturdy point of view, in contrast to "Presentism"—my view, at least in the essentials.[9]

Eternalists were given a boost by the *seeming* implications of relativity, which *seemed* to permit the conceptualization of a "timescape," laid out at once, with the so-called future as real as any other part of the construction. The gauntlet was hurled by a British philosopher in 1908. J. M. E. McTaggart was his name and the title of his influential essay was "The Unreality of Time."[10]

McTaggart worked out a critique of the past-present-future understanding of time that made it seem so absurd—so full of contradictions of a *logical* nature—that it made no sense.

The furor over the claims of the philosophic Eternalists has continued right down to the present.[11]

Those who were convinced by McTaggart overruled their own experience of time. They were dazzled by logic. And it has to be admitted that McTaggart's performance was effective. He was good with paradox.

He acknowledged the obvious sequence—the progression—from before to after that is integral to human experience and seems in ontological terms to be *immediate*. He called this the "A series" of phenomena—the series that is full of contradictions. He called it *illusion*, while acknowledging the obvious fact that for some strange reason it *exists*. He also posited a "B-series" that constitutes the deeper and more fundamental reality that contradicts time—the *real* reality. He even posited a "C series" to account for the mysterious way in which "A" coexists with "B."[12]

This is the Eternalist doctrine, as it carries over into "block-time" theory, and the proposition that "time never passes" is an issue that carries great weight to this day among philosophers and physicists.[13] But the "Presentist" response is inevitable.

McTaggart and friends regarded logic as sufficient, but it isn't—not for this challenge. It doesn't help us come to terms with the experience that frames all the others: the mystery of *now*.

If time is an illusion, our experience of *now* is illusion—and where does that leave us? The experience of *now* contains the essence of our very own selfhood—our essence of *life*—the life we are *living*.

Again we return to the philosophic fundamentals, for the quest of McTaggart—and his *geste scandaleux* of 1908 was merely symptomatic of a broader and more fundamental quest—arose from the age-old search for the realities that stay and abide while all the transient things of this world evanesce and go away. That was what his time-critique was all about. The impetus behind it goes back to Parmenides and Plato.

We inhabit the zone of the middle dimensions, so-called, in which our senses serve our daily needs. Beyond are the things that we will never understand—like the secret ontology of time.

If we think philosophically—or mystically—we wish to know these things for *what they are*.

And so we stretch our mental powers just as far as they can go in our quest to know and understand. But the secrets that intrigue us must remain forever out of reach—just beyond our grasp.

Is this acceptable?

Not for some: some people find the situation so outrageous they embrace dogmatic theology. And they seek revelation with a fiery fervor that can leave no place for any doubt. None at all.

William James, in his classic study of religious emotions and sensibilities—for he did great work in psychology along with his important contributions to philosophy—discussed the "instability" of people whose religion "exists not as a dull habit, but as an acute fever." He observed that

> invariably they have been creatures of exalted emotional sensibility. Often they have led a discordant inner life, and had melancholy during a part of their career. They have known no measure, been liable to obsessions and fixed ideas; and frequently they have fallen into trances, heard voices, seen visions, and presented all sorts of peculiarities which are ordinarily classed as pathological. Often, moreover, these pathological features in their careers have helped to give them their religious authority and influence.[14]

This certainly applies to the people who refuse to say the words "I don't know" when confronting the ineffable—those mysterious things that lie beyond our ken and that no human being ever grasps. No, they refuse to admit it—they *push on*, leaping every single hurdle with passion to *believe*, and they *strive* to the point of reaching certitudes that neither they nor anyone can prove.

They insist upon them anyway.

Even lofty philosophers are not immune from such "fever," though its symptoms are subtle compared to the behavior of soapbox exhorters. What they do is intellectual—and yet their feelings can be every bit as powerful as those of the people who are openly and fervently religious.

The commonality among these metaphysical seekers—though they sometimes quarrel with each other—is basic, since they all seek the kind of total certitude that the normal facts of life rule out. There is a *bond* among these personality types, and so their operating methods are similar.

As a matter of course—once they are believers—they will sometimes proclaim that the things we perceive are unreal. Their purpose is naturally to clear away a vista for their own revelation of the "real."

And this is what happened in the case of McTaggart, whose *purposes* determined his logic. His contention that time is an illusion was a warm-up for what was coming next: his declaration that reality consists of pure "souls" that coexist forever, a doctrine he expounded at length in the aftermath of his 1908 essay.

An atheist, he arrived at such a quasi-religious construction in his quest to know and understand. The force behind his logic must without a doubt have been emotional. He was human—like the rest of us.

So much for his Eternalism and the purpose that determined its logic— its logical *agenda*. The skepticism he employed in his encounter with the time phenomenon flipped without missing a beat into certitude when he changed the subject to his own hypothetical version of "reality."

He was one of those people who cannot live at peace within the limits of what our minds can know. He made claims that could never be proven after making his name as a *logician*. Here without question is an object lesson when it comes to the larger mysteries pertaining to ontology and mind.

Any mysticism that is *realistic* must shun leaps of faith when they masquerade as certitude. That is how the human mind can go terribly wrong, and we can see the effects every day.

Those of us who are candid have nothing to do with false certitude—if we can help it. We affirm just a few propositions: (1) we are a part of a larger reality, (2) we know this through our own self-awareness, (3) this awareness is grounded in our minds, and (4) these exist within the process of *now*.

That is *all*.

But in truth it is enough, for our minds possess the power to accomplish quite a lot that is thrilling.

We can measure the velocity of galaxies racing away from one another. We build spacecraft. We can peer down at viruses and figure out ways to disable them. Are these "illusions?" Of course not. There is a ghostly dimension to the way that we are doing these things—ghostly, in the medium of time—and the realities we know will keep melting away into the past. But through the miracle of *now* we get to *do these things*, and thus achieve our own kind of glory. That is part of what *now* means for us; it is *immediate*—we *know* it—and it gives us all the power we need.

It is also the calling card of cosmological mystery—the sign of Being that we rightly hold in awe. It is real—and we need to insist upon this in response to the people who deny it. We should take another moment to consider that issue, for if *now* is inauthentic, the ontology of mind is incoherent.

Let us hear once again from the scientific skeptics who invoke relativity against us—those who call the experience of *now* inauthentic since no present moment can exist throughout the whole cosmos.

Here is the example from a previous chapter: the problem of time "dilation" in the spaceship. If a person on a superfast spaceship ages more slowly than the rest of us do, it makes no sense to ask what the astronaut might be doing "at the present moment"—that is, now—because the astronaut's "*now*" is very different from our own and the future that he thinks he is approaching cannot correlate with ours.

So what? The situation amounts to just this: "present moments" (plural) in the cosmos are *out of synchronization* with each other since space-time is flexible—it can "warp." But this in no way disproves the authenticity of *now* as an ontological *fact*.

Discrepancies between cosmic laws and the *reality* we know are not resolved by dismissing our experience—especially if that experience is universally shared. The answer will be found in *hidden* laws. Even physicists who say that the passage of time is an illusion must look at their watches now and then.

They admit it.

If "*now*" is an illusion—nothing more than a construction of our minds—we are led to the strange and entertaining doctrine of "solipsism": the notion that nothing external to ourselves can be proven to exist. For all we know, the solipsist would say, the "real world" that we think we behold is a will-o'-the-wisp that we ourselves are creating.

The doctrine of block time leads to solipsism for this reason: our immediate experience of *now* is not only a condition of our own *self-awareness*—a sense that is internal to our minds—it is the ground for our perception of *all other things*, and this includes the *external realities*. If our sense of *now* is an illusion, then *our knowledge of the outside world is illusion* since our knowledge of *anything* must be filtered through the ontological medium of *now*. There is no escape.

Now is essential to our own sense of Being, and if our sense of Being is some kind of an illusion, it is certainly a very strange illusion since it begs the obvious question of who—or what—is the entity, the center of awareness, that is being deceived.

How can anything constitute *illusion* without something *real* that is being *deceived*? Our minds (among other things) *exist* and our selfhood is *real*.

The block-time people need to give their own account of what they think is really going on. They seldom try.

No, it appears that our experience of *now* may be the foremost object of certitude we have, for our minds are *embodied right in it*. There is *one dispensation*—one force above others that can guarantee their actuality.

For a long time—at least since Plato—philosophers have frequently concluded that we grasp no more than the appearances of things and the reality "behind" these appearances is hidden. Immanuel Kant laid down the clear distinction between "phenomena" (appearances) and "noumena," which are "things in themselves." And the things in themselves, he believed, are completely unknowable.[15]

Even our own self-awareness (apperception) is nothing but appearance, according to Kant.[16]

Of course, this begs the question of what the "appearance" is being presented to—what *sees* it. What constitutes the center of awareness that we know—this *thing* that we regard as our "self?" What supports it?

We did not create ourselves, and we do not sustain the fact of our existence. There is something "*behind*" our existence that is making us *real*, some *power* that is *giving* us our lives. Where is it? We feel it—somehow—but it eludes us the more we try to grasp it. It is elsewhere. Or could it be that this "something *behind* our existence"—this thing-in-itself—is also … *in us*?

It must be *here*—whatever it is—to *support* our existence, must it not?

A number of philosophers took up the challenge of *explaining* the *Ding an sich*—the thing-in-itself, or whatever equivalent notion fit into their ontology. Schopenhauer arrived at the conclusion that the universal essence is "Will."[17] Other philosophers presume that their theories can never advance beyond the level of mere "phenomenology."[18]

But our experience of *now* should make us wonder. Could it be that in this one single case—this *ontic* case—the realms of noumena and phenomena overlap so completely that the gap has been effectively bridged? Consider: our experience of *now* is both phenomenal (a feeling in our minds) and noumenal in that it manifests the locus, the ontological ground, the undeniable sine qua non of our Being … *immediate Being.*

For we are indisputably *here*. Heidegger's term for our experience of being-ness was "*Da*sein": being *there*.

Let posterity ponder that issue.

In the meantime, let us thrive all we can in the immediate *now*—eternally *with* us.

EPILOGUE

I was raised in the Jewish tradition.

When I was young, I found the services at our synagogue extremely impressive. This was a "Reformed" congregation, so the services were perforce in English and I could understand them easily. The Rabbi was extraordinarily eloquent. I still remember his name: Norman Gerstenfeld.

Over time, however, I found that my Jewish heritage meant less to me as I questioned a great many things. My parents encouraged me to think for myself, and so I did. My interest in religious issues—I felt prompted to ask the great question: Why does anything exist instead of nothing?—demanded more than I could find in any program of this fine congregation. The sermons dealt with ethics and not metaphysics. I needed more. I was looking for answers to much bigger questions than the sermons ever really addressed. I felt a sense of ennui as I listened to the biblical legends of the ancient Hebrews and their doings.

In time I became an agnostic.

But then, on my thirteenth birthday in 1963—the age 13 is the time for one's Bar Mitzvah—John F. Kennedy's life was blown away, and the world that I knew was smashed apart. Kennedy 's reputation among the historians as well as in popular culture rises and falls. I regard him as a very great leader, and my reasons are explained in a book that I wrote back in 2010, *Lincoln's Way*. But whatever the verdict on his policies—as well as on the racy details of his life—his influence for good upon American *culture* was and is indisputable. His humor, intelligence, and charm ushered in a true age of good feelings in America—short-lived though it was. His banter with reporters at his televised press conferences seemed magical to me. His shrewd judgment interspersed with mischievous fun set an admirable tone for public life—for millions of people. I was lucky, I knew, to be living in days such as these—days with this exuberance filling the air.

In an instant, all that was gone. I learned a quick and terrible lesson: life is precious and appallingly fragile. This blithe and gifted man was blown away in mere seconds by a miserable, inscrutable wretch.

From that point on I felt a sense of resolute purpose, and I swore that I would never waste a day. I do not mean to give the impression that I sank into a hyper-serious state: far from it. I could laugh at myself and be mischievous just as much as ever. But I would never forget what I had learned on November 22, 1963.

I would strive to make my dreams (the good ones, of course) come true if I possibly could. If not, I would still have the comfort of looking back and saying, "I left nothing undone—or untried." I remembered a motto that Kennedy had shared in one of his final press conferences: the way to live the good life, he observed, is to make "full use of your powers along lines of excellence."

Fast forward many decades to my recent past: at age 65, I was suddenly diagnosed with stage 2 cancer. I was cured, but the emergency gave me a late-life reprise of the shock that I experienced in 1963. The following statement, as cancer lore goes, is without a doubt extremely trite, but its content for me remains strong: I was conscious as never before that every single day is a gift. The message of this book began to dawn upon me: every moment we live we are *upheld* by stupendous power. As never before, I was aware of the ghostliness and splendor of *now*.

So I decided to live in it—play in it—marvel at it every day as I went about my business.

I do not live purely "in the moment" in the sense that I disregard the past and the future. That's impossible. And it is nothing that anyone should try—if they are wise enough to heed common sense. I bask in my memories (the good ones) and look over the horizon toward tomorrow. And I always keep a weather-eye open as I scan the horizon for danger.

But I am mindful of the wonder of *now*. Some would say that this experience is all that we have, and in a certain sense they would be right. We can always remember and anticipate. But the gift of *now* is all we have. And that's my own day-to-day religion—my creed in this adventure of life.

It is enough.

APPENDIX A

THE REALITY ON *NOW* AS AN ONTOLOGICAL CONDITION

In this appendix we return to the examination of *now* as an ontological issue that calls for analysis.

It is very significant that physicists have worked out geometries such as "world lines" to "*locate events*" in the fabric of space-time using mathematics.[1] The impulse to *locate* derives from an experience that all of us share. But its source is ontology, the nature of being, and every physicist would certainly benefit by pondering this, and so would we.

For the conceptions of *now* and *location* relate to each other in a way that sheds light upon reality.

Prepare to spend a minute or two with these questions and do not be in a hurry as you do so. Take your time as you scrutinize the following distinct propositions.

Here are two related propositions—both derived from philosophers and physicists. One: *now* is *illusion*. If our experience of *time* is an illusion, our experience of *now*—which *flows*—is illusion. Two: *location* is *real*.[2]

Now examine these thoughts as they affect one another: *now* is an illusion, but *location* is real. Does this concoction make any sense at all? Think it over as a matter of ontology: the mystery of what it means to "be."

The *being* of events requires *location*, which is more than just a matter of *space* because the cosmos is integrated *space-time*. No "pure and simple space" can exist in a universe like this one.

"Location" must also be *specific*—just as *definite* in everyday experience for us as being *here* and not anywhere else. And this requires a dimension of *real* temporality that manifests its presence as *now*.

Real temporality—one that makes itself constantly apparent as we work and play "here and now."

Thus location is determined in *both* space and time—as they are focused in the medium of *now*. The principle of *now* is nothing less than *inherent* in the fact of "location" as we know it.

Consider a quick illustration. "We're at this place *now*," we may say to ourselves, and yet the place is very different from the place that we experienced *before*. It may look and feel "the same," and yet it isn't. The place *as it was* no longer exists—it has melted away into the past.

Is that not so?

As we experience *now*, we are part of a *holistic* presence: the *unfolding* of the day-to-day world. And there's the "explicate order" as envisioned by Bohm—the blossoming of things—the *becoming*.

We are moving toward a vision of *now* that goes far beyond the notion that it represents an aspect of time. It may be something much greater than that: it may constitute the substance of the world.

Who can say?

It is *now* that determines all location in the human experience—that much is clear. So it is not just a quality of time. *It is a power that binds space and time.* It is *around* us as well as within.

It is therefore not an illusion.

Events in their nature must derive from a deeper metaphysical basis—a deeper source of being. Those who dismiss our experience of *now* as an illusion are pulling the rug from under their very own feet—saying things that lack intelligibility. For this state of our existence is *something*.[3] And *now* is the standpoint from which we can experience *anything*, including ourselves. *It is integral to any location.* To call *now* an illusion just misses the point of the issue: the issue of Being.

But we are still not finished with the ontological question, for the *quantum* issue will affect it.

Physicists say that we are living in a "zone of middle dimensions"—a zone that our senses can explore.[4] Our perception of ourselves and of the world must be conditioned by the terms of this zone. No other conditions are accessible to us with the senses that we normally employ.

And this means that our time-sense is not really false, as some physicists suppose—it is *true* within the bounds of this *zone*.

But science has revealed to us that very different senses are required by the quantum enigma. Far "below" us is a very different zone—a zone of subatomic mystery—that science probes with specialized equipment.

In the quantum reality "particles" are "neither here nor there." No one can track them with precision. Their "particle" behavior is also the behavior of a *wave*, so their *locations* can be only *approximate*.

Fritjof Capra once put it this way: "The particle has tendencies to exist in various places and thus manifests a strange kind of physical reality between existence and non-existence."[5] Robert Oppenheimer toyed with his readers as he expounded the principles of quantum uncertainty as follows:

> If we ask [...] whether the position of the electron remains the same, we must say "no;" if we ask whether the electron's position changes with time, we must say "no;" if we ask whether the electron is at rest, we must say "no;" if we ask whether it is in motion, we must say "no."[6]

Very funny, but the point for ontology is serious. Propositions regarding *location* have become problematical.[7]

And this affects our conception of *now*.

We are *changing*—there is no doubt about it—and our lives are ever-changing *events*. We will never know what happened to the "self" that we experienced a mere half-second ago. It is *gone*.

But for all that, we know that we are *here*. We are *here* in this changing "here and now"—whatever that is.

Let's view it like this: *here* is our immediate location in the overall reality of *now*. Does that work?

THE ONTOLOGICAL COMPLEXITIES OF *NOW*

A QUANTUM MODEL

The reality of *now* is apparent, but its ontological nature is hard to articulate.

The crux of the matter is the problem I endeavored to finesse when I used the term "liquid clarity" for *now* as we know it through experience. Our existence is *definite*, and yet it moves in a never-ending *flow*, and this generates a dazzling array of conceptual challenges, both ontological and scientific.

Alfred North Whitehead in *Process and Reality* offered ontological principles for his "organic" philosophy. "Continuity," he wrote, "concerns what is potential, whereas actuality is incurably discrete."[1]

Whitehead's units of existence, his so-called actual occasions, represent the *actualizing* of potential. But if applied to the *now* situation, any actualization is ipso facto a component of a larger continuity.

The physicist Henry Stapp has striven to synthesize Whitehead's ontology with quantum theory. In Stapp's system, every "actual occasion" is a moment when a "quantum leap" occurs; that is, a *selection* takes place among a cloud of innumerable potentialities. This selection results in a "reduction" or "collapse" event that eliminates every one of the possibilities that were not selected.

And every time this occurs, a new "general quantum state" of the entire universe is born.

N*ow* is defined by Stapp as "the (space-like) three-dimensional surface" at which the "reduction" or "collapse" events happen. But this "surface" is a *flow* that stretches out—*melts forward*—and so the problems of defining its temporal boundaries and internal structure are daunting.

Stapp conceptualizes the moving potentialities arriving at the threshold of *now*, so to speak, and then he speaks of "the initial NOW" as the receiving point for these potentialities. At "some stage" of this process, a "quantum 'reduction' event occurs"—a selection is made among the cloud-like range of possibilities—and this selection "is associated with a certain mathematical 'projection' [...] that acts directly not only on the new part of the current surface NOW, but indirectly (via entanglement) on the entire surface NOW, at least in principle."[2]

These terms—the initial NOW, the new part of the current surface NOW, and the entire surface NOW—make it clear that this "surface" is an oscillating state in which events are localized only in part. Stapp makes provision for uneven properties of *now* in light of the inherent nature of quantum indeterminacy—in other words, *freedom*.

What this means, paradoxically, is that *now* will encompass a fluctuating *swath* of "present moments." Each one of them consists of a quantum reduction event, and they keep changing the general composition of *now*.

In a figure that accompanies his text, Stapp represents *now* as a wavy line with a froth of events bubbling upward. Stapp explains that "the wavy line [...] represents some initial surface" of *now*—let us notice the fact that we are speaking here of *some* initial surface rather than *the* initial surface. Stapp continues, "This surface pushes continuously forward" as reductions occur in different regions of space-time.

Every one of these reductions causes indirect changes in other parts of *now*. The events are irregular, because of the nature of quantum indeterminacy. And they all change the wavy surface instantly.

The problem becomes more complex when "relativistic" considerations are brought into play and the *now* situation is applied to the extended (and inherently curved) construction of space-time—the construction in which any "localized" events will have indirect ramifications throughout a *now* surface that is presumably copresent in very distant regions. This means that every quantum event will immediately ramify across the wavy surface of *now* to the outer limits of the cosmos.

Stapp puts it this way: the "direct changes" represented by a local reduction event will generate "indirect changes along the rest of the surface" (i.e., *now*) "due to quantum entanglements." And "these 'indirect changes' must logically produce the sort of faster-than-light effects that Einstein dismissed as 'spooky actions at a distance.' "[3]

They must be faster-than-light (i.e., instantaneous) because they apply in a *now*-surface that is omnipresent, notwithstanding the fact that its "present moments" are out of temporal synchronization due to the paradoxes of relativity, such as the phenomenon of time dilation with increases in velocity.

The possibility of faster-than-light effects is presumably dead-on-arrival in the world of science because the principles of special relativity were confirmed so early and so often in famous experiments. But the mathematics of the quantum theory have also been confirmed, and the ontological implications of the quantum system require us to consider the possibility of faster-than-light transmission. Stapp explains:

> If, at some instant, nature makes a choice of response to a probing action that is localized in some confined spatial region then, according to the basic quantum rules, the quantum state of the entire universe changes not just in that local region, but all over 3D space at that instant of time.[4]

And though "the founders of quantum mechanics did not want to admit or suggest that, in defiance of the theory of special relativity, information could *really* be transmitted faster-than-light," that possibility must indeed be considered:

> Given the validity of some basic macroscopic predictions of quantum mechanics, there is no way that the macroscopic phenomena can conform to the predictions of quantum mechanics without allowing violations of the general notion that the information about the local free choices cannot get essentially instantaneously to far-away regions and affect outcomes appearing in those regions.[5]

NOTES

PREFACE

1 Sweeney's rebellion began with her revolt against the Catholicism in which she was raised. The literature of "recovering Catholics" is filled with poignancy. An interesting comparison to Sweeney's confession may be found in the book *When God Is Gone Everything Is Holy: The Making of a Religious Naturalist* by science writer Chet Raymo.

2 John P. Gulliver, "A Talk with Abraham Lincoln," New York *Independent*, September 1, 1864.

3 Fritjof Capra, *The Tao of Physics: An Exploration of the Parallels between Modern Physics and Eastern Mysticism* (Boulder, CO: Shamhala, 1975), 2010 edition, 11, 44, 191.

4 Ibid., 27.

CHAPTER 1. TOWARD A SPIRITUALITY OF INDEPENDENT THINKING

1 In 1952, Bertrand Russell stated the issues with admirable sarcasm as follows:

> If I were to suggest that between the Earth and Mars there is a china teapot revolving about the sun in an elliptical orbit, nobody would be able to disprove my assertion provided I were careful to add that the teapot is too small to be revealed even by our most powerful telescopes. But if I were to go on to say that, since my assertion cannot be disproved, it is intolerable presumption on the part of human reason to doubt it, I should rightly be thought to be talking nonsense. If, however, the existence of such a teapot were affirmed in ancient books, taught as the sacred truth every Sunday, and instilled into the minds of children at school, hesitation to believe in its existence would become a mark of eccentricity and entitle the doubter to the attentions of the psychiatrist in an enlightened age or of the Inquisitor in an earlier time. It is customary to suppose that, if a belief is widespread, there must be something reasonable about it. I do not think this view can be held by anyone who has studied history.

Bertrand Russell, "Is There a God?," in John G. Slater (ed.), *Last Philosophical Testament, 1943–68* (The Collected Papers of Bertrand Russell: Volume II), London: Routledge, 1997), 547–48.

2 Robert Green Ingersoll, "Why Am I Agnostic?," *North American Review*, vol. 149 (December 1, 1889), 741–49. Ingersoll's article appeared only one year before the publication of Sir James G. Frazer's classic anthropological study *The Golden Bough*, which surveyed primitive superstitions and myths underlying religion. The book subverted Christianity by showing the prevalence around the world of rituals involving a god who, in human incarnation, must be slain and then resurrected.

3 David Hume, "The Dialogues Concerning Natural Religion (1779)," in Charles W. Hendel, ed., *Hume Selections* (New York: Charles Scribner's Sons, 1927), 284–401.

4 William James, *The Varieties of Religious Experience, Being the Gifford Lectures on Natural Religion Delivered at Edinburgh in 1901–1902* (London: Longmans, Green, 1902, 1958 Mentor edition), 391.

5 Martin Heidegger, *An Introduction to Metaphysics*, Ralph Manheim, trans. (New Haven, CT: Yale University Press, 1959), 1.

6 Ibid., 18–19.

7 Saint Augustine, *Confessions* (AD 397–400), R. S. Pine-Coffin, trans. (New York: Penguin Books, 1961), 267, 269.

8 The Chandogya Upanishad (ca. 500 BC), Part 6, chapter 2, in Swami Nikilandanda, *The Upanishads: A New Translation* (New York: Ramakrishna Vivekanada Center, 1986), 294.

CHAPTER 2. METAPHYSICS, PHYSICS, AND THE SPIRITUALITY OF *NOW*

1 In quantum mechanics, elements of indeterminacy are combined with elements of regularity. In the 1920s, physicists Erwin Schrödinger and Louis de Broglie suggested that subatomic particles partake of wave-like qualities that render their movement in the aggregate "probable" rather than definite. Physicist Brian Greene explains the nature of the mathematics as follows: "It was not long before Schrödinger's equations and the probabilistic interpretation were being used to make wonderfully accurate predictions." But these were predictions that suggested where particles *might* appear *most* of the time, and the contingency within these probabilities remained very strange. Greene continues:

> According to quantum mechanics, the universe evolves according to a rigorous and precise mathematical formalism, but this framework determines only the probability that any particular future will happen—not which future actually ensues. […] Everyone agrees on how to use the equations of quantum theory to make accurate predictions. But there is no consensus on what it really means to have probability waves, nor on how a particle "chooses" which of its many possible futures to follow, nor even on whether it really does choose or instead splits off like a branching tributary to live out all possible futures in an ever-expanding arena of parallel universes.
>
> Brian Greene, *The Elegant Universe: Superstrings, Hidden Dimensions, and the Quest for the Ultimate Theory* (New York: Random House, 1999), 107.

2 The origins of string theory derived from a problem in reconciling the mathematics of relativity and the mathematics of quantum mechanics. Each system generated a coherent body of mathematics that could be tested and confirmed. The problem was that the two systems were sometimes difficult to reconcile. By the 1970s, the new conception of string theory presented a way to synthesize the mathematics of relativity and quantum mathematics. The conception of 11-dimensional microcosmic space can be traced back to 1919 when the German mathematician Theodor Kaluza suggested the possibility of more than just three spatial dimensions. In 1926, the Swedish mathematician Oskar Klein theorized that additional space dimensions may include both "extended" dimensions and microcosmic "coiled-up" or circular dimensions. The "Kaluza-Klein" theory was revived in the 1970s by the early string theorists, who developed the concept of elementary units of the cosmos that rotate and vibrate in multidimensional "curled-up" space. A six-dimensional construction was pioneered by mathematicians Eugene Calabi and Sing-Tung Yau. The "Calabi–Yau Space" was eventually extended to 11 possible dimensions and this became essential to the mathematics of string theory. In 1995, the physicist Edward Witten suggested that the different variations of string theory covered different but related variations of a single underlying problem, so he coined the term "M-theory" for the overall school of thought. His choice of the letter M was rather gnomic and some suggested that the letter should signify "magic" or "mystery."

3 Saint Augustine, *Confessions* (AD 397–400), R. S. Pine-Coffin, trans. (New York: Penguin Books, 1961), 267, 253.

4 Saint Thomas Aquinas, *Summa Contra Gentiles* (ca. AD 1260), in *Aquinas: Selected Philosophical Writings*, Timothy McDermott, trans. (Oxford: Oxford University Press, 1993), 276.

5 See Adam Frank, "Three Theories That Might Blow Up the Big Bang," *Discover*, March 25, 2008, accessible via https://www.discovermagazine.com/the-sciences/3-theories-that-might-blow-up-the-big-bang.

6 See J. Richard Gott and Li-Xin Li, "Can the Universe Create Itself?," *Physical Review D*, May, 1998, accessible via https://www.scribd.com/document/78707522/J-Richard-Gott-III-and-Li-Xin-Li-Can-the-Universe-Create-Itself.

7 Thomas Torrance, *Divine and Contingent Order* (Oxford: Oxford University Press, 1981), 36.

8 Paul Davies, *The Mind of God: The Scientific Basis for a Rational World* (New York: Simon & Shuster, 1993), Touchstone edition, 171. See also Lawrence M. Krauss, *The Universe from Nothing: Why There Is Something Rather than Nothing* (New York: Free Press, 2013).

9 David Bohm, *Wholeness and the Implicate Order* (London: Routledge, 1980).

10 Henry P. Stapp, *Mindful Universe: Quantum Mechanics and the Participating Observer* (Berlin: Springer-Verlag, 2007), 92.

11 Martin Heidegger, *Being and Time* (1927) John Macquarrie and Edward Robinson, trans. (New York: Harper & Row, 1962), Harper Perennial edition, 475.

12 Paul Davies, *About Time: Einstein's Unfinished Revolution* (New York: Simon & Schuster, 1995), Touchstone edition, 258.

13 Einstein wrote this statement in a letter of consolation to the widow of his friend Michele Besso after the latter's death in March, 1955. See *Albert Einstein-Michele Besso Correspondence, 1903-1955*, Pierre Speziali, ed. (Paris: Hermann, 1972), 538.

14 Albert Einstein, quoted in *The Philosophy of Rudolf Carnap*, P. A. Schilpp, ed. (La Salle, IL: Open Court, 1963), 37.

CHAPTER 3. WHY IS THE WORLD THE WAY IT SEEMS?

1 Alfred North Whitehead, *Process and Reality* (1929), David Ray Griffin and Donald W. Sherburne, eds. (New York: Free Press, 1978), 350.

2 Everett was inspired by the speculations of physicist Richard Feynman, who theorized that with infinite time and infinite space, every possible sequence of events must at some point exist through quantum creativity.

3 Davies, *The Mind of God*, 216.

4 Ibid. One thing about which *orthodox* quantum physicists (those who follow the schematic created by John von Neumann) agree is that every quantum event creates a "collapse" or "reduction" (i.e., destruction) of the other possibility sets, and that a new "quantum state" is thus established throughout the entire universe. The many-worlds theory is *non*-orthodox, since its scheme rules out destructive "collapses" because *all* possibilities are actualized in different universes. As pointed out in the text, this theory is *deterministic*, whereas orthodox quantum theory is very much the reverse.

5 Davies, *The Mind of God*, 217.

6 Eugene Mallove, "The Universe as Happy Conspiracy," *Washington Post*, October 27, 1985, B-2.

7 Whitehead, *Process and Reality*, 345, 349–51.

8 Immanuel Kant, *Critique of Pure Reason* (1781), Norman Kemp Smith, trans. (New York: Macmillan, 1929), St. Martin's Press edition, 396–97.

9 Ibid., 77.

10 Hermann Weyl, *Philosophy of Mathematics and Natural Science* (Princeton, NJ: Princeton University Press, 1949), 166.

11 J. J. C. Smart, "Time and Becoming," in *Time and Cause*, P. van Inwagen, ed. (Reidel: Dordrecht, 1980), 3–15.

12 David Park, "The Myth of the Passage of Time," *Studium Generale*, vol. 24 (1971), 20.

13 Roberto Mangaveira Unger and Lee Smolin, *The Singular Universe and the Reality of Time* (Cambridge: Cambridge University Press, 2015), xi.

14 Not the least of the problems with this system is the issue of "infinity" in understanding *now*. Barbour imagines a perfect inventory of *nows* in Platonia, where every possibility subsists. The appeal of this vision derives from the fact that every *now* is supposed to be *definite*. But is it? As any number can be subdivided endlessly, the contents of *now* (for all we know) may be *endlessly divisible*. The quantum "possibilities" within it (even if considered as frozen abstractions) may stretch to "infinity" in different dimensions. This situation frustrates the side of our nature that longs to give everything a final and crisp "definition." One of our most important and easily overlooked mental foibles is to look for a *sharp-edged focus* in our conceptualizing, and this tendency can be useful. But it can also be taken too far and distort our better judgment. Ambiguity and indeterminacy should be as real to us as clarity.

15 Julian Barbour, *The End of Time: The Next Revolution in Physics* (Oxford: Oxford University Press, 1999), 49.

16 Smolin worked with Barbour early in his career and the two of them were co-authors. But though Smolin gave Barbour's book *The End of Time* consideration—to the point of writing a dust-jacket endorsement—he eventually rejected Barbour's reasoning. See Lee Smolin, "The Unique Universe," *Physics World*, June 2, 2009, accessible via https://physicsworld.com/a/the-unique-universe/.

17 Barbour, *The End of Time*, 28.

18 William James, *Pragmatism* (1907), in *Pragmatism and Four Essays from the Meaning of Truth* (Cleveland: Meridian Books, 1955), 45.

19 John G. Bennett, "What Is Time?" *Systematics: The Journal of the Institute for the Comparative Study of History, Philosophy, and the Sciences*, vol. 1, no. 2 (September, 1963), 180–81. Speculation regarding the existence of multiple time dimensions has necessarily included the possibility of circular time dimensions. And the perennial doctrine of "eternal recurrence"—a feature of several religious belief systems that has also been pondered by philosophers from Pythagoras to Nietzsche as well as by countless occultists—is based on the concept of circular time. Brian Greene has discoursed on the current speculation among physicists who see circular microcosmic time dimensions as a possible extension of the 11-dimensional space construction of string theory:

> If a curled-up dimension is a time dimension, traversing it means returning, after a temporal lapse, to a prior instant in time. This, of course, is well beyond the realm of our experience. Time, as we know it, is a dimension we can traverse in only one direction with absolute inevitability, never being able to return to an instant after it has passed. Of course, it might be that curled-up time dimensions have different properties from the familiar, vast time dimension that we imagine reaching back to the creation of the universe and forward to the present moment. But, in contrast to extra spatial dimensions, new and previously unknown time dimensions would clearly require an even more monumental restructuring of our intuition. Some theorists have been exploring the possibility of incorporating extra time dimensions into string theory, but as yet the situation is inconclusive.

Greene, *The Elegant Universe*, 6, 205.

20 Heidegger, *Being and Time*, 278, 488.

21 David Kyle Johnson, "Does Free Will Exist?" *Think*, Vol. 14, no. 42 (2016), 9.

22 Paul Davies, *God and the New Physics* (New York: Simon & Schuster, 1983), Touchstone edition, 97.

23 Ibid., 115. For an interesting demonstration of the fact that many scientists are open-minded when it comes to this issue, see Andrea Lavassa, "Free Will and Neuroscience: From Explaining Freedom Away to New Ways of Operationalizing and Measuring It," *Frontiers in Human Neuroscience*, June 1, 2016, US National Library of Medicine, National Institutes of Health, accessible via https://www.ncbi.nlm.nih.gov/pmc/articles/PMC4887467/ and Stuart Hameroff, "How Quantum Brain Biology Can Rescue Conscious Free Will," October 12, 2012, *Frontiers in Integrated Neuroscience*, accessible via https://www.ncbi.nlm.nih.gov/pmc/articles/PMC3470100/.

24 Davies, *God and the New Physics*," 115.

25 Henry P. Stapp, *Quantum Theory and Free Will: How Mental Intentions Translate into Bodily Actions* (Berlin: Springer International, 2017), xi.

26 Henry P. Stapp, *Mind, Matter, and Quantum Mechanics* (Berlin: Springer-Verlag, 2009), 3.

27 David Hume, *An Enquiry Concerning Human Understanding* (1777), Eugene Freeman, ed., (LaSalle, IL: Open Court Classics, 1966), 39.

28 John Locke, *An Essay Concerning Human Understanding* (1690), Alexander Campbell Fraser, ed. (New York: Dover, 1959), II, 222, 260, 262.

29 James Jeans, *The Universe around Us* (New York: Macmillan, 1929), 128.

30 Whitehead, *Process and Reality*, 19, 56, passim.

31 Davies, *The Mind of God*, 232.

32 Paul Davies, "Does Matter Have a Mind of Its Own?" *Washington Post*, June 12, 1988, C-3.

33 Harold J. Morowitz, *The Emergence of Everything: How the World Became Complex* (Oxford: Oxford University Press, 2002), 193.

34 Paul R. Fleishman, *Wonder: When and Why the World Appears Radiant* (Amherst, MA: Small Batch Books, 2013), 287.

35 Ibid., 9.

36 Davies, *The Mind of God*, 185.

37 Alfred North Whitehead, *Science and the Modern World* (New York: Macmillan, 1925), 249.

38 Stapp, *Mindful Universe*, 20.

CHAPTER 4. FREEDOM, SPIRITUALITY, AND STRUGGLE

1 Whitehead, *Process and Reality*, 178. The roster of philosophers and scientists who have embraced or at least flirted with pan-psychism constitutes a very long list. The notion was widespread among the pre-Socratics, especially in the doctrines of Anaxagoras, Anaximenes, and Heraclitus. Plato embraced it at least to the extent that he theorized an "anima mundi" that pervades the emanations from the realm of Pure Ideas. In the Renaissance, theoreticians like Gerolamo Cardano, Giordano Bruno, and Francesco Patrizi endorsed it. Patrizi gave the doctrine its name: pan-psychism. Later Leibniz and Schopenhauer worked out their own distinct variations and several American pragmatists worked out versions of pan-psychism before the famous endorsement of the doctrine by William James. Alfred North Whitehead, Carl Jung, and the physicist Arthur Eddington joined the roster in the early twentieth century. In recent decades, the following authors and their works have been influential in advancing different versions of pan-psychism: Thomas Nagel, "Pan-Psychism" (1979), David Bohm, "A New Theory of the Relationship of Mind and Matter" (1990), David Chalmers, *The Conscious Mind* (1996), and Galen Strawson, "Realistic Monism: Why Physicalism Entails Pan-Psychism" (2006). The variation of the theory that envisions a latent *potential* for mind—without necessarily attaining full consciousness—throughout the universe is sometimes called "panprotopsychism."

2 Arthur Schopenhauer, *The World as Will and Representation* (1818), E. F. J. Payne, trans. (New York: Falcon's Wing Press, 1958), 1969 Dover Publications edition, 411–12.

3 Arthur O. Lovejoy, *The Great Chain of Being: A Study in the History of Ideas, the William James Lectures Delivered at Harvard University*, 1933 (Cambridge: Harvard University Press, 1936), 30.

4 Martin Heidegger, *Being and Time*, 210, 219–24.

5 Paul Davies, *About Time*, 174–75.

6 Ibid., 175.

7 Ibid., 181.

CHAPTER 5. THEOLOGY AND WORSHIP

1 James, *The Varieties of Religious Experience*, 396.

2 Ibid.

3 Dudley Fitts, *Aristophanes: Four Comedies*, New English Versions (New York: Harcourt, Brace & World, 1962), 307.

4 George L. Mosse, *The Crisis of German Ideology: Intellectual Origins of the Third Reich* (New York: Grosset & Dunlap, 1964), 116.

5 Reinhold Niebuhr, *The Children of Light and the Children of Darkness* (New York: Charles Scribner's Sons, 1944), 10–11.

6 *Chuang Tzu: Genius of the Absurd*, trans. James Legge, arranged by Clae Waltham (New York: Ace Books, 1971), chapter 17, quoted in Capra, *The Tao of Physics*, 115, also accessible via http://www.100jia.net/texte/zhuangzi/zhuangzilegge1.htm.

7 Lovejoy, *The Great Chain of Being*, 26, 24.

8 *Bhagavad Gita*, chapter 9, lines 7–8, Juan Mascaro, trans. (New York: Penguin Classics, 1964), accessible via https://iefworld.org/cmpBhagavadGita_env.html.

9 Heidegger, *Being and Time*, 481.

10 Ibid., 482.

11 James Joyce, *A Portrait of the Artist as a Young Man*, (New York: Viking Press, [1916] 1957), 168–71.

12 See Garth Fowden, *The Egyptian Hermes: A Historical Approach to the Late Pagan Mind* (Cambridge: Cambridge University Press, 1986).

13 Maurice Nicoll, *Living Time and the Integration of Life* (London: Vincent Stuart, 1952), 261, 262, 277.

14 John G. Bennett, *The Dramatic Universe* (London: Hodder & Stoughton, 1956).

15 Gustaf Strömberg, *The Soul of the Universe* (Philadelphia, PA: David McKay, 1940).

16 For an extended study of this movement, see my book *Love in the Afterlife: Underground Religion at the Movies* (Madison, NJ: Fairleigh Dickinson University Press, 2016). Critical Reactions to some of these productions bear witness to their spiritual impact. In response to John Balderston's play *Berkeley Square*, the movie critic of the *New York Herald Tribune* called it "the most important play of the season" due to its "intellectual qualities," its "fascinating metaphysical conception of time," and its "moving emotional values." The *London Times* reviewer wrote that "there is magic in this play, enough to set it apart from all the common traffic of the theatre, and to send dreams scudding in the wake of dreams." For a manifesto of the literary movement that glorified the mystical qualities of time, see J. B. Priestley, *Man and Time* (London: Aldus Books, 1964).

17 Eckhart Tolle, *The Power of Now: A Guide to Spiritual Enlightenment* (Vancouver: Namaste Publishing and New World Library, 1999), 18.

18 Ibid., 13.

19 Ibid., 48–50.

20 Ibid., 83.

21 Ibid., 219–20. Tolle recounts the way in which he first found peace, the transformative experience that led to the method he later developed. The psychiatric implications of the following are obvious:

> Until my thirtieth year, I lived in a state of almost continuous anxiety interspersed with periods of suicidal depression. [...] One night not long after my twenty-ninth birthday, I woke up in the early hours with a feeling of absolute dread. [...] The silence of the night, the vague outlines of the furniture in the dark room, the distant noise of a passing train—everything felt so alien, so hostile, and so utterly meaningless that it created in me a deep loathing of the world. The most loathsome thing of all, however, was my own existence. What was the point in continuing to live with this burden of misery? [...] I could feel that a deep longing for annihilation, for nonexistence, was now becoming much stronger than the instinctive desire to continue to live. "I cannot live with myself any longer." This was the thought that kept repeating itself. [...] Then suddenly, I became aware of what a peculiar thought it was. "Am I one or two? If I cannot live with myself, there must be two of me: the 'I' and the 'self' that 'I' cannot live with." "Maybe," I thought, "only one of them is real." I was so stunned by this strange realization that my mind stopped. I was fully conscious, but there were no more thoughts. Then I felt drawn into what seemed like a vortex of energy [...] I heard the words "resist nothing," as if spoken inside my chest. I could feel myself being sucked into a void. It felt as if the void was inside myself rather than outside. Suddenly, there was no more fear.

When he awoke, everything seemed "fresh and pristine, as if it had just come into existence. I picked up things, a pencil, an empty bottle, marveling at the beauty and aliveness of it all. [...] For the next five months, I live in a state of uninterrupted deep peace and bliss" (ibid., 3–5).

CHAPTER 6. THE MISUSE OF SPIRITUALITY

1 Karen Armstrong, *A History of God: The 4,000-Year Quest of Judaism, Christianity and Islam* (New York: Ballantine Books, 1993), xvii.

2 Ibid., xxi.

3 Ibid., 397.

4 Ibid., 394.

5 See Joseph Margolis and Tom Rockmore, eds., *Heidegger and Nazism* (Philadelphia: Temple University Press, 1990).

6 Heidegger, *An Introduction to Metaphysics*, 199.

7 Thomas Mann, *The Coming Victory of Democracy* (New York: Alfred A. Knopf, 1938), 14. I have often thought that this 1938 book might well have been part of the inspiration for the 1939 film *Mr. Smith Goes to Washington*, produced and directed by

Frank Capra, who went on to produce the "Why We Fight" series of training films in World War II.

8 Ibid., 22.

9 Ibid., 24.

10 Ibid., 23–24.

11 Ibid., 14.

12 Erich Fromm, *The Anatomy of Human Destructiveness* (New York: Holt, Rinehart & Winston, 1973), Fawcett edition, 246.

13 Ibid., 369, 366.

14 As to the identity of John the gospel writer, "tradition" identifies him as one of the original disciples of Jesus, but some believe he was a different man who produced the text at a much later date and then allowed himself to be misidentified as "the beloved disciple" of Jesus to lend his text more authority. For commentary on this possible deception, see Hugh J. Schonfield, *Those Incredible Christians* (New York: Bernard Geis Associates, 1968), Bantam edition, 192–97.

CHAPTER 7. PARADIGMS OF GOD

1 Armstrong, *A History of God*, 399, 397.

2 *Enneads* of Plotinus (ca. AD 270), Richard Emil Volkmann, ed. (Leipzig: Teubner, 1884), V, 4, 1, quoted in Lovejoy, *Great Chain of Being*, 62.

3 Alexander Pope, *An Essay on Man* (1733), in John Butt, ed., *The Poems of Alexander Pope* (New Haven, CT: Yale University Press, 1963), 513: 237–40.

4 Armstrong, *A History of God*, 243–52, 266–71.

5 Schonfield, *Those Incredible Christians*, 242–58.

6 Friedrich Wilhelm Joseph von Schelling, "Über das Wesen der menschlichen Freiheit" (1809), in *Schellings Werke* (Leipzig: F. Eckardt, 1907), III, 499, translated by Arthur O. Lovejoy in *Great Chain of Being*, 318.

7 Henri Bergson, *Évolution créatrice*, Arthur Mitchell, trans. (New York: Henry Holt, [1907] 1911), 247.

8 Against a Jesuit critic who argued that his metaphysics were pantheistic, Bergson replied in 1912 that he conceived of God as the *source* of the life force that is *distinct* from the force itself. But when Bergson wrote that God "*is* unceasing life, action, freedom," he surely blurred any possible theistic distinction between creator and creation. Arthur O. Lovejoy later observed that Bergson simply

> gives the name of God to the inexhaustible reservoir of vital energy in which he believes; but he warns us that we must not be misled by the figure—the reservoir is not a receptacle containing this energy, it is not a reserved quantity of life force kept temporarily in an inactive condition until it is needed; it is just the endless "shooting out" of life itself, regarded as inexhaustible.

Arthur O. Lovejoy, *The Reason, the Understanding, and Time* (Baltimore, MD: Johns Hopkins Press, 1961), 181–82.

9 William Blake, *Songs of Innocence and Experience*, in Ruthven Todd, ed., *Blake, Selected Poetry* (New York: Dell, 1960), 81.

10 Amid the immense wealth of commentary on these issues of Buddhism, it is interesting to read the commentary of the Dalai Lama on the Heart Sutra. See the Dalai Lama, *Essence of the Heart Sutra: The Dalai Lama's Heart of Wisdom Teachings*, Geshe Thupten Jinpa, trans. (New York: Simon & Schuster, 2002). For an interesting psychological commentary on Sunyata metaphysics, see David R. Loy, "Avoiding the Void: The Lack of Self in Psychotherapy and Buddhism," *Journal of Transpersonal Psychology*, vol. 24, no. 2 (1992), 151–80, accessible via http://enlight.lib.ntu.edu.tw/FULLTEXT/JR-ENG/loy8.htm.

11 Davies, *God and the New Physics*, 18.

12 John Russell Wheeler with Kenneth Ford, *Geons, Black Holes, and Quantum Foam: A Life in Physics* (New York: W. W. Norton, 1998), 351.

13 John Wilmot, Earl of Rochester, *Upon Nothing*, in David M. Vieth, ed., *The Complete Poems of John Wilmot, Earl of Rochester* (New Haven, CT: Yale University Press, 1968), 118.

14 Davies, *God and the New Physics*, 19. J. B. Priestley commented in *Man and Time* on this issue as follows:

> We have been compelled to become more and more aware of smaller and smaller divisions of time. How often have I heard, when recording for radio, somebody say "We'll begin—in ten seconds from *now*." And there are still hundreds of millions of people in the world who would not be able to understand that sharpened *Now*. In the advanced science and technology of our own age, even a second can be regarded as a great clumsy piece of time, so that it is divided by a thousand—into *milliseconds*. Now it could be argued that when a *millisecond* means something, when we are aware of smaller and smaller time divisions, we ought to be expanding and enriching our experience, and, for all I know, this may be true for the eager experimenters who play with *milliseconds*. It is not yet true for all the people outside labs. (163)

15 Bryce DeWitt, "The Many-Universes Interpretation of Quantum Mechanics," in B. d'Espagnat, ed., *Foundations of Quantum Mechanics* (Cambridge: Academic Press, 1971), quoted in Davies, *God and the New Physics*, 116.

16 Davies, *God and the New Physics*, 117.

CHAPTER 8. MYSTICISM

1 Capra, *The Tao of Physics*, 42.

2 See, for example, Fred Alan Wolf, *The Dreaming Universe: A Mind-Expanding Journey into the Realm Where Psyche and Physics Meet* (New York: Simon & Schuster, 1994); Wolf, *The Spiritual Universe: One Physicist's Vision of Spirit, Soul, Matter, and Self* (Portsmouth, NH: Moment Point Press, 1996); Joseph Selbie, *The Physics of God: Unifying Quantum Physics, Consciousness, M-Theory, Heaven, Neuroscience, and Transcendence* (Newburyport, MA: New Page Books, 2018); and Paul Levy, *The Quantum Revelation: A Radical Synthesis of Science and Spirituality* (New York: Selectbooks, 2018).

3 Davies, *God and the New Physics*, 215.

4 Ibid., 34.

5 Ibid., 55–56.

CHAPTER 9. A PATH OF ONE'S OWN

1 Rousas John Rushdoony, *By What Standard? An Analysis of the Philosophy of Cornelius Van Til* (Vallecito, CA: Ross House Books, 1995), 24; Rushdoony, *The Institutes of Biblical Law* (Phillipsburg, NJ: Presbyterian and Reformed, 1973), I, 30.

2 Rousas John Rushdoony, *Intellectual Schizophrenia: Culture, Crisis, and Education* (Phillipsburg, NJ: Presbyterian and Reformed, 1961), 100.

3 Rushdoony, *Institutes of Biblical Law*, I, 286.

4 Armstrong, *A History of God*, 283.

5 Ibid., 311.

6 Ibid., 307.

7 Ibid., 286.

8 Ibid.

9 Ibid.

10 Ibid., 378.

11 Ibid., 383.

12 Ibid., 316.

13 Paul Davies, *God and the New Physics*, 1.

14 Ibid., 4–5.

15 Ibid., 3.

16 Ibid., 7.

17 John Maynard Keynes, *Newton, the Man*, Royal Society of London "Newton Tercentenary Celebrations, 15 July 1946" (Cambridge, UK: Cambridge University Press, 1947), 27, 34. The manuscript of Keynes's 1942 talk was presented by his brother Geoffrey Keynes at the Royal Society proceedings in 1947. Examples of religious sensibilities that have found a powerful gratification in science could be piled up easily. Here is an interesting example: Frederick T. Gates, a former Baptist minister who became the chief of philanthropic operations for John D. Rockefeller Sr., who was himself a fervent Baptist. Under Gates's leadership, Rockefeller founded and endowed the Rockefeller Institute for Medical Research (RIMR), today's Rockefeller University, which specializes in advanced medical science. After touring the institute and gazing through microscopes, Gates told Simon Flexner, the institute's director, that "to you He is whispering His secrets. To you He is opening up the mysterious depths of His Being. There have been times when, as I looked through your microscopes, I have been stricken with speechless awe. I felt that I was gazing with unhallowed eyes into the secret places of the Most High." Ron Chernow, *Titan: The Life of John D. Rockefeller, Sr.* (New York: Random House, 1998), 476.

18 Chet Raymo, *When God Is Gone Everything Is Holy: The Making of a Religious Naturalist* (Notre Dame, IN: Sorin Books, 2008), 16.

19 Davies, *God and the New Physics*, 8, ix.

CHAPTER 10. ONTOLOGY AND MIND

1 See Arthur O. Lovejoy, *The Revolt against Dualism: An Inquiry Concerning the Existence of Ideas* (London: George Allen & Unwin, 1930), 222–56. Lovejoy's espousal of "psychophysical dualism" was argued at the expense of Bertrand Russell's

"monism," which Lovejoy subjected to a logic-based refutation that was rather old-fashioned in light of the emergence of quantum physics, which he tried to handle with the same sort of logical devices later in the book. But 90 years after the publication of *The Revolt against Dualism*, the enigmas of the quantum world remain resistant to classical logic. Though Lovejoy argued for a stark bifurcation of nature—through which mind is a realm that is separate from physical space-time—it may be possible that monism and dualism are true in simultaneous senses. The psychophysical *synthesis* recently described by Henry P. Stapp (see note 8) resolves many of the difficulties in Lovejoy's arguments. In Stapp's view, the mental and physical realms are connected through quantum states and through emergence. Pan-psychism is the surest foundation for such speculation regarding the way of such things in this cosmos, and Lovejoy was a skeptic—or at least an agnostic—regarding the theory. In response to Sir Arthur Eddington's suggestion that the "indicator readings" of cosmic reality are linked to a "background" with a "nature capable of manifesting itself as mental activity," Lovejoy wrote that it was best to "proceed upon the hypothesis that the cosmical background is of a non-mental sort or to admit our ignorance of its nature," in other words to leave "the background of the perceptible world indeterminate, if we must" (*The Revolt against Dualism*, 270–71, 273). Problems such as these present further illustrations of the way that philosophy can push our powers to their limits. Take, for example, the issue of qualities like color or musical tones. Does the "redness" we know when we see something red have its own distinctive niche—a *physical* niche—within the space-time containing our brains? Pan-psychism forces us to change our way of thinking about that problem. In Stapp's theory of dipolar quanta (see note 8), mind and brain coexist, and so the basic terms of reference are changed. In this view, every part of our mental life—our abstract thoughts, computations, and even our fantasies—exist within space-time. But take "redness" as an "essence," a self-subsistent abstraction, a "thing in itself" that can stand somehow "on its own." Can it possibly exist within space-time? Philosophy has given us a different way of handling that problem: the concept of "subsistence," as opposed to "existence." See C. E. M. Joad, *Guide to Philosophy* (London: Victor Gollancz, 1936), Dover edition, 262–67. Some philosophers have gone further and consigned things like "redness" to a higher metaphysical plane *above* space-time, a realm of subsistent "Ideas" in the Platonic sense. Alfred North Whitehead found this view convincing. And he probed the subject in unusual ways, such as this: "We know about the color 'green' in some of its perspectives. But what green is capable of in other epochs of this universe, when other laws of nature are reigning, is beyond our present imaginations." Alfred North Whitehead, *Modes of Thought* (New York: Macmillian, 1938), Lecture III, 59.

2   Douglas Hofstadter, *Gödel, Escher, Bach: An Eternal Golden Braid* (New York: Basic Books, 1979), 709.

3   Fleischman, *Wonder: When and Why the World Appears Radiant*, 46.

4   John William Dunne, *An Experiment with Time* (London: A. & C. Black, 1927), Hampton Roads edition, 97.

5   Amid the considerable literature on this subject, a good summation may be found in Philip Ball, "The Strange Link between the Human Mind and Quantum Mechanics," February 16, 2017, BBC/Earth, accessible via http://www.bbc.com/earth/story/20170215-the-strange-link-between-the-human-mind-and-quantum-physics.

6 Freeman Dyson, *Disturbing the Universe* (New York: Basic Books, 1979), 249.

7 Morowitz, *The Emergence of Everything*, 101.

8 Stapp, *Mindful Universe*, 96. Stapp has offered a schematic version of the synthesis, which he acknowledges is still incomplete. He writes:

> In the Whiteheadian ontologicalization of quantum theory, each quantum reduction event is identified with a Whiteheadian actual entity/occasion. Each Whiteheadian actual occasion/entity has a "mental pole" and a "physical pole." There are two kinds of actual occasions. Each actual occasion of the first kind is an intentional probing action that *partitions* a continuum into a collection of discrete experientially different possibilities. Each actual occasion of the second kind selects (actualizes) one of these discrete possibilities and obliterates the rest. According to this Whiteheadian quantum ontology, objective and absolute actuality consists of a sequence of psychophysical quantum reduction events, identified as Whiteheadian actual entities/occasions. These happenings combine to create a growing "past" of fixed and settled "facts." Each "fact" is specified by an actual occasion/entity that has both a physical aspect (pole) and a mental aspect (pole), and a region in spacetime from which it views reality.

Stapp goes on to theorize that every physical pole has a mathematically described "input" and "output." The input of the physical pole draws from "physically described state of the universe" on the threshold of *now*. The mental input draws from all the mental outputs of previous occasions. He continues:

> The process by which the mental and physical inputs are combined to produce mental and physical outputs involves, according to Whitehead, aspects identified as appetites, evaluations, and satisfactions. Thus idea-like qualities are asserted to enter into the dynamics of the basic process that creates the actual occasions, and hence reality itself. The paradigmatic example of an actual occasion is an event whose mental output is an addition to a human stream of conscious events, and whose physical output is the actualized neural correlate of that mental output. (96–97, 90)

If this theory proves to have demonstrable applicability, two metaphysical questions (probably unanswerable) remain: how do the two kinds of actual occasions work in unison and what does the "continuum" of possibilities that they manipulate consist of?

9 When they use the term "Presentism," some philosophers mean to assert that only "the present" is "real." In my view, allowance must be made for the way in which "the past" *subsists* via memory, historical facts, and perhaps in other ways. Here again, however, as previously argued, the secret metaphysics of time cannot be fathomed by our minds. But Stapp's analysis, in note 8, is a valiant attempt to sketch the concepts.

10 J. M. E. McTaggart, "The Unreality of Time," *Mind*, vol. 17 (1908), 457–73. McTaggart was an atheist and a proponent of philosophic idealism who believed in the reincarnation of immortal souls. His doctrine of the unreality of time was developed at greater length in his multivolume work *The Nature of Existence*, which was published posthumously in 1927 by Cambridge University Press. Though an atheist, his vision of a "B-series"—a duration that contains all temporal reality—was a secularized version of the Augustinian/Thomistic doctrine that God perceives all things "at once" in a single gaze. God, wrote Thomas Aquinas, "stands on the summit of eternity where everything exists together, looking down in a single simple glance on the whole course of time." (Thomas Aquinas, *In Aristotelis Librum Peri Hermeneias,* in *Aquinas: Selected Philosophical Writings,* 282). This concept laid the groundwork for modern philosophic idealism. In the eighteenth century, George Berkeley argued that the world is Idea and that the gaze of an Absolute Mind confers reality upon it. McTaggart converted this vision from theistic to atheistic terms.

11 Bertrand Russell, a pupil of McTaggart's, flirted with Eternalism without fully embracing it. Cambridge philosopher Charlie Dunbar Broad embraced Eternalism in 1921 but repudiated it in 1923, when he stated that his theory of time "accepts the reality of the present and the past, but holds that the future is simply nothing at all." (C. D. Broad, "Time," in, J. Hastings, et al., eds., *Encyclopedia of Ethics and Religion* (Edinburgh: Charles Scribner's Sons, 1923), XII, 66). Later in life, he propounded the doctrine that time is "absolute becoming," a "continual supersession" of "phases." (C. D. Broad, "Autobiography," in P. A. Schlipp, ed., *The Philosophy of C.D. Broad* (New York: Tudor, 1959), 766). Contemporary critics of Eternalism or block-time theory are legion. They include the philosopher John Lucas, the physicist Lee Smolin, and the physicist and philosopher Avshaom Elitzer, among many others. The physicist Paul Davies struggled with the "time problem" and the "now problem" at length in his book *About Time: Einstein's Unfinished Revolution.* As a physicist, he was troubled by the "disconnection" between our mental *sensation* of time and the inability of physics to generate the kind of data that are needed to corroborate that sensation as an accurate understanding of cosmic reality. And so he struggled to align his thinking with the "block-time" school of thought that took its cues from Einstein. At one point, he proclaimed that "Einstein scuttled the idea of a universal now, and pointed the way to 'block time,' in which all events—past, present and future—are equally real. To the physicist, human beings of the twenty-fifth century *are* 'there.' [...] They are there—*in the future!*" (260). But it was no use: he could not make himself believe such things, and so he had to admit that "as a human being, I find it impossible to relinquish the sensation of a flowing time and a moving present moment" (275). Therefore, he concluded that the very parameters of inquiry in the field of physics must be fundamentally deficient: "We are missing something important from the physics of time and our perception thereof" (276). The following conclusion seems justified: our immediate experience of time is authentic within our particular zone of experience. But there are obviously other zones—"below" us and "above" us—that put time in a perspective that our minds cannot fully understand. As to relativity and the proposition that the future "already exists," the mathematician Hermann Bondi put his finger on the essential problem by observing that block-time theory is *deterministic* and leaves out the concept of freedom, which the findings of quantum physics demand—or *seem* to demand. "The flow of time," he wrote, "has no significance in the logically fixed pattern demanded by deterministic theory, time being a mere coordinate. In a theory with indeterminacy, however, the passage of time transforms the statistical expectations into real events." See Hermann Bondi, "Relativity and Indeterminacy," *Nature,* vol. 169 (1952), 660. Many physicists and philosophers have observed that the outlook of Einstein was in many respects deterministic. For commentary, see Lawrence W. Fagg, *The Becoming of Time: Integrating Physical and Religious Time* (Durham, NC: Duke University Press, 2003).

12 In some respects, McTaggart's "B-series" corresponds to the aboriginal concept of "eternal dream time" that anthropologists have reported in their studies of Australian aboriginal culture. In eternal dream time, the sequence of our waking time dissolves into a presentational field in which all time is copresent, and totemistic rituals are used in efforts to usher the minds of participants into this state or purported state. See A. P. Elkin, *The Australian Aborigines* (New York: Anchor Doubleday, 1964). Comparable constructions (with admittedly significant variations) may be found in the doctrine of Parmenides, in many of the orthodox monotheistic conceptions of God, especially those of St. Augustine and St. Thomas Aquinas, the vision of Alfred North Whitehead who spoke of the way things "perish, yet live forevermore" in the substance of God, and in esoteric lore—especially so in the concept of the "eternal Now" developed by Maurice Nicoll, in the so-called eternity axis of John G. Bennett, and other formulations of participants in "the Work," as described in Chapter 5. All of these related visions flow from deep and fundamental human longings. It should go without saying that the power of the human mind to validate such ideas amounts to nothing. There has been a great deal of disputation among philosophic Eternalists as to the true nature of a "B-series," for the notion of "atemporality" can of course be construed in a multitude of ways, and while disputes of this kind are in a sense quite genuine and interesting, they are also inherently sterile because mere *games* cannot deliver reliable knowledge or prove much of anything.

13 The proposition of "block time" in physics is illuminated by controversies in philosophy that are comparable in certain respects because they center on assertions that "before" and "after" may be absent in some forms of "duration." An exchange of views between the philosophers Henri Bergson and Arthur O. Lovejoy on the nature of duration illustrates the delicacies of time metaphysics in a controversy that seeks to explore these conceptual issues with the utmost seriousness. The illustration of a musical melody is offered as an object for analysis. Bergson:

> You will be able to have a clear feeling of all this if, while listening to a melody, you allow yourself to be lulled by the sound—at the same time making abstraction from all the visual images which, in spite of yourself, will tend to modify the auditory perception—visual images of notes of music written on paper, or musical instruments beginning and ceasing to play, etc. You will become conscious that the melody progresses, that it is a movement or a change, that it is a thing which lasts, and which, consequently, is not a simultaneity; but that, in this melody, the past is incorporated with the present, and constitutes with it an indivisible whole. It is only by an effort of reflection that, subsequently turning back upon this indivisible whole once constituted, you represent it to yourself as a simultaneity, because of its indivisibility— which leads you to have a spatial image of it, capable of being cut up into distinct terms, decomposable into a "before" and "after," which then would be juxtaposed. No doubt this melody, even in pure duration, seems divisible in the sense that at any given moment it would come to a stop; but if it actually came to a stop, we should have a different melody, which would itself be indivisible. When we pronounce a phrase all at once, without punctuation, we have, once more, the clear feeling of a succession without before and after, the feeling of a *solid*—by which I mean an indivisible—duration. [...] Our inner life, from the beginning to the end, is thus an indivisible continuity, and it is this that I call our duration. It is succession, but succession without distinct and numerical multiplicity, that is to say, *pure* duration.

Lovejoy:

> For myself, I can only say that I have never experienced a melody in which the notes had no "distinct and numerical multiplicity," or were not apprehended as in the relation of "before" and "after." I seem to myself, indeed, to hear each separate note, one after the other, though, while hearing each, I may be continuously aware of the total musical unit, or pattern, of which it is a part. If the melody is wholly new to me, I do not become aware of this pattern in its entirety until the last note sounds, unless, when the melody has partly run its course, I seem to "catch" it by anticipating, perhaps erroneously, the notes I have not yet heard. That Bergson's experience was really the same seems implied by his remark that "at any moment the melody may come to a stop; but if it actually came to a stop, we should have a different melody." Only a *sequence* of which the units are experienced as before and after one another *can* "come to a stop"; a temporally "indivisible" unity would have all its elements present at once, and there could be no question of stopping, or not stopping.

And thus more generally, Lovejoy argued as follows:

> It is only to particulars that the terms past, present, and future have any relevance at all. And to play fast and loose with these terms, when speaking of *one and the same particular*—i.e., to say that a particular specified as past with respect to another specified as present, is also compresent *with* the latter—is manifestly to falsify the fact of experience.

Such a falsification "is repugnant to the very essence, not only of intelligible discourse, but of coherent thought." Lovejoy never had occasion to comment on the "block-time" argument that dispenses with the terms past, present, and future altogether. But the gist of his thinking on the problem of temporality would seem to apply to it. Lovejoy, *The Reason, The Understanding, and Time*, 185–87, 192–93, 196–97.

14 James, *The Varieties of Religious Experience*, 24–25.

15 Kant's doctrine of "noumena" has been the subject of controversy for a long time, not least of all because it was inconsistent. On the one hand, he argued that we lack the power to know anything at all about noumena. On the other hand, he imputed very definite qualities to noumena, among them timelessness and freedom. Since noumena have nothing to do with time—which is just an "inner sense" or appearance, according to Kant—they are "free," whatever that means. But he never explained what this "freedom" amounts to or how noumena *use* their freedom since *action* requires a sequence of before and after. Kant struggled with these issues in his *Critique of Practical Reason*, and the results were unsatisfactory.

16 Kant, *Critique of Pure Reason*, 167–68. Kant discoursed upon the problem as follows:

> How the "I" that thinks can be distinct from the "I" that intuits itself […] and yet, being the same subject, can be identical with the latter; and how, therefore, I can say: "I, as intelligence and *thinking* subject, know myself as an object that is *thought*, in so far as I am given to myself as something other or beyond that which is given to myself in intuition, and yet know myself, like other phenomena, only as I appear to myself, not as I am to the understanding"— these are questions that raise no greater nor less difficulty than how I can be

an object to myself at all. [...] So far as inner intuition is concerned, we know our own subject only as appearance, not as it is in itself.

In a sense Kant was right, for we can never know the full truth about what is "going on" within the process that constitutes our identity. In a different sense, however, he was wrong, insofar as our immediate awareness of selfhood is more than just *appearance*, for whatever "appearance" of ourselves may appear to our minds, there is something within us that is *seeing* this appearance, and that "something" is completely *immediate*.

17 As for Schopenhauer's duality of "Will and Representation"—*Wille* und *Vorstellung*—he made it clear that the latter was not exactly a counterpart to Kant's term "phenomenon" or "appearance," but rather the aspect of the world through which it is "knowable" to thinking subjects. Insofar as Schopenhauer sought to define the *Ding an sich*, he insisted it could only be conceived or apprehended as a *two-sided thing*. He put it this way:

It is necessary to consider separately the side of the world from which we start, namely the side of the knowable, and accordingly to consider without reserve all existing objects [...] merely as representation. [...] That from which we abstract here is invariably only the *will*, as we hope will later on be clear to everyone. This will alone constitutes the other aspect of the world, for this world is, on the one side, entirely *representation*, just as, on the other, it is entirely *will*. But a reality that is neither of these two, but an object in itself (into which also Kant's thing-in-itself has unfortunately degenerated in his hands), is the phantom of a dream, and its acceptance is an *ignis fatuus* in philosophy.

Schopenhauer, *The World as Will and Representation*, 4.

18 For a moving demonstration of the impulse to try to probe beyond appearances in order to apprehend "noumenal" realities, consider this discourse of Herman Melville's Captain Ahab, who, like Kant, distinguished a thing-in-itself behind appearances, but who, like Schopenhauer, regarded this force as essentially evil:

All visible objects, man, are but as pasteboard masks. But in each event—in the living act, the undoubted deed—there, some unknown but still reasoning thing puts forth the mouldings of its features from behind the unreasoning mask. If man will strike, strike through the mask! How can the prisoner reach outside except by thrusting through the wall? To me, the white whale is that wall, shoved near to me. Sometimes I think there's naught beyond. But 'tis enough. He tasks me; he heaps me; I see in him outrageous strength, with an inscrutable malice sinewing it.

It bears noting that however pathological the zeal to probe to the heart of reality may become—however much it may lead the fanatic into "leaps of faith" that generate dogma—our longing to probe beyond appearances is in no way absurd if we acknowledge our limits. In fact, it is potentially the basis for a very sane spirituality. The opposite tendency—to *shun* all forms of speculation (*overt* speculation of a serious nature)—has led some philosophers in recent times to stunt their intellectual lives. The sterility of "logical positivism" in the early to mid-twentieth century provides a case in point, and so does the contemporary culture of "phenomenology," which is sterile in very different ways. There is nothing inherently wrong with the phenomenological methods if sincere curiosity suffuses them. Heidegger showed the way to make use of phenomenological techniques as a pathway to fundamental ontology. But too often in contemporary studies, "phenomenology" devolves into word games that are largely self-referential and lacking in seriousness—in *gravitas*. Its practitioners—whose adherence to the folkways of this school can become a kind of reverential conformity—forget that they are part of a *movement*, phenomenol*ism*, that rests upon premises as questionable as those of most other philosophic movements, whether realism, idealism, positivism, pragmatism, or any other. This is especially true in the work of Jean Paul Sartre, his many successors, and the philosophic schools that they created. I find the work of Sartre unintelligible, and it must be remembered that he did most of his writing under the influence of amphetamines.

APPENDIX A: THE REALITY ON NOW AS
AN ONTOLOGICAL CONDITION

1 The concept of "world lines" was developed in the first decade of the twentieth century by the mathematician Hermann Minkowski, a teacher of Einstein's who developed the concept of "space-time" in response to Einstein's theory of special relativity. World lines are geometrical diagrams depicting the paths of event-progressions through the multifaceted curvatures of the cosmos. A "light cone" is a concept that derives from the Minkowski geometries. "Events" in the light-cone model are locations that occur in the converging and diverging trajectories of particles and waves. Depending on their speed—be it the speed of light or any slower speed—causal processes can relate to "events" in a pattern with a cone-like geometrical shape.

2 According to Sir Arthur Eddington, the system of Minkowski for ascertaining cosmic location "is a way of keeping accounts of space" that is "true [and] exhibits realities (absolute things)." Eddington, *The Nature of the Physical World* (New York: Macmillan, 1928), 34.

3 The following proposition appears to me self-evident: scientific experiments can never probe the nature of ontic conditions, for those very conditions are the *pre*conditions that control the experiments themselves. We can never "get outside" of the cosmic reality to study it in ways that do not partake of its nature.

4 Capra, *The Tao of Physics*, 64.

5 Ibid., 154.

6 Robert Oppenheimer, *Science and the Common Understanding* (New York: Oxford University Press, 1954), 42–43.

7 Whitehead wrote at length in the 1920s on the "fallacy of simple location."

APPENDIX B: THE ONTOLOGICAL COMPLEXITIES
OF NOW: A QUANTUM MODEL

1 Whitehead, *Process and Reality*, 61.

2 Stapp, *Mindful Universe*, 94.

3 Ibid. For the most thorough exploration of these topics to date, see Michael Epperson, *Quantum Mechanics and the Philosophy of Alfred North Whitehead* (New York: Fordham University Press, 2004).

4 Stapp, *Quantum Theory and Free Will*, 46.

5 Ibid., 46, 48, 91.

INDEX

Lightning Source UK Ltd.
Milton Keynes UK
UKHW010215011021
391401UK00001B/90

9 781839 981258